Help for the Co.  ..hy

How to Use a ..ac:
a guide for windows computer users

by Michael Gorzka
mike@computershy.com • www.computershy.com
Illustrations by Charissa Wilson
www.TripleLatteDesign.com

HELP! for the

"Computer shy"

1

Introduction

"Make it like the Mac!" has always been Microsoft's mantra.

The general misconception seems to be that Windows and Mac computers are worlds apart. This is not at all the case.

Microsoft has always tried (unsuccessfully) to emulate the look and feel of the Mac.

The bottom line is that if you can use a Windows computer then you will certainly be able to take full advantage of everything that Mac computers have to offer in a *very short period of time.*

Many people are understandably apprehensive about making the switch from the problematic (but familiar) Windows Operating System to the Mac platform.

In fact, the anxiety that many people have expressed to me over the last couple of years by the very *thought* of switching to the Mac actually inspired the creation of this book.

The good news is that there's nothing to be nervous about!

Despite the numerous advantages that Mac computers have over Windows PCs, both types of computers *operate pretty much the same way.*

Basically if you can point & click the mouse and use a computer keyboard, you're golden!

Part of Apple's loyal following has been due to the fact that Mac computers have a smoother *look and feel* than Windows computers.

Unlike other computer manufacturers, Apple makes not only *computer hardware* but also the *Operating System* (Mac OS X) and various *software programs* (Apple Safari, TextEdit, Apple Mail, iWorks, iTunes, etc.) to run on that hardware.

This enables the unique *Mac experience* to be created --- an experience that you may well get addicted to over time.

I do my best to carefully describe the basic operations of a Mac computer and to teach the operations of the various Mac Computer programs.

But please also watch the visual demonstrations that come with this book. They will reinforce the material that we cover here.

You'll find the Mac movies at http://gallery.mac.com/ help4computershy.

I will also be adding *additional Mac computer visual demonstrations*. Please subscribe to the free Help for the Computer Shy newsletter to be notified when they are posted.

If you have any problems with downloading the Mac videos and/or viewing them, please give me a yodel at mike@computershy.com.

Administrative User Account

 Apple Computers are built around **security**. When you set up a new Mac computer you will have to select an *Administrator password.*

You will need to verify your Administrator password before you can:

- Install 3rd party software on your Mac
- Install system & program updates from Apple
- Create & edit "User Accounts"
- Set up Parental Controls

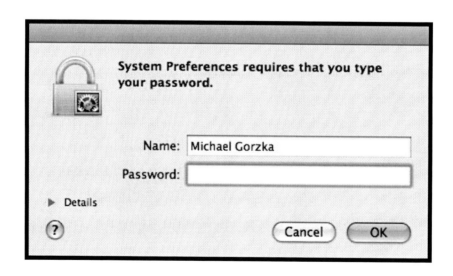

In short, whenever you want to do something that could potentially harm or compromise the security of your Mac (such as downloading new software), you will have to type in your Admin password.

As already stated, you will select an Admin password for yourself when you first set up your new Mac.

The first time you turn on your new Mac computer, you will see a series of screens that will prompt you to type in information such as your name, language preference, email address, street address, and the **Admin password** that you will use to *administrate* your Mac computer.

These registration screens are pretty straightforward.

If you are familiar with using a Windows computer (which I assume you are since you are reading this book), you should have no problems with the Mac registration procedure.

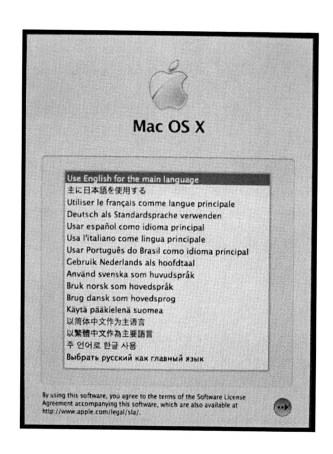

Please proceed slowly and carefully as you complete the Mac registration process.

If you have any questions about your Mac computer setup, email me at mike@computershy.com.

 Just as a suggestion, before you begin the Mac registration / personalization procedure, you may want to read the "Introducing... the Apple Mouse" chapter for a quick primer on how to use the one-button Apple Mouse.

If you have trouble remembering passwords, you may want to write down the Administrator password that you select and keep it in a safe place.

Better yet, write down your *password hint* and keep it in a safe place.

My password hint for example is "first cat's name and the year of Dad's birth".

Passwords are cAse seNsiTive and never have spaces in them.

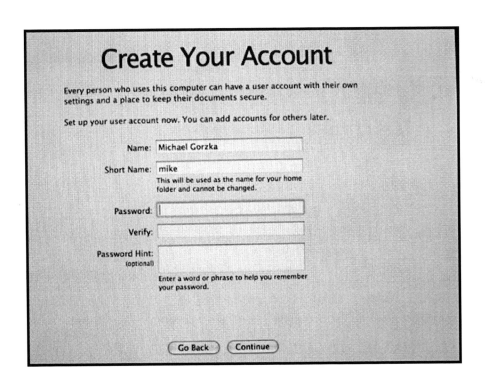

Introducing.... the Apple Computer Mouse

The Apple Computer mouse operates very much like a Windows Computer mouse --- with a couple of minor differences.

First and foremost, the Apple Mouse has only one mouse button on the top.

Clicking either side of the Apple mouse has the same effect.

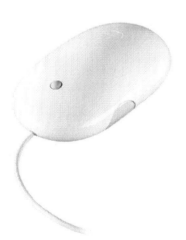

The buttons on the sides of the mouse can be *programmed* to do such things as trigger your Mac's "Expose" feature or instantly reveal your Mac desktop.

What if I need to click the *right side* of the mouse?

If you need to click the right side of the mouse (such as when you want a pop-up menu to appear), you can "simulate" a right mouse click by *holding down* one of the "control" keys on the bottom row of your computer keyboard as you are clicking the mouse.

What does the "little ball" at the top of the mouse do?

Pressing the little ball (by default) causes your dashboard "widgets" to appear (an outrageously fun topic that we explore in a later chapter). This action can be changed, however.

I really miss the two-sided mouse! Can I use a two-sided mouse with my Mac?

Yes, you can buy a **USB** two-sided mouse and use that instead.

But just as a suggestion, you may want to give the Apple mouse a chance. It's elegant and can be programmed to do some very useful things. Plus it's part of the Apple computer experience!

When should I single-click the mouse and when should I double-click the mouse?

Double-click the mouse to start programs from within the Applications folder and to open windows & folders.

For everything else, a **single mouse click** should suffice (including starting a program from the program dock).

I've seen a lot of people over the years *double-click* the mouse unnecessarily.

This makes your computer work harder and inflicts more wear and tear on your wrist.

The Apple Computer Keyboard

 The Apple Keyboard works very much like a Windows computer keyboard with just a few (but important) differences.

For example, pressing the "F11" key on the top row of your Apple Computer keyboard will reveal your Mac Computer Desktop.

Pressing the "F9" key will reveal all the windows that you currently have open (in neat little rows).

Pressing the "F12" key will cause your dashboard widgets to appear.

The Apple computer keyboard also has three keys on the bottom row which Windows computers do not have.

These keys will at first be a bit alien to an experienced Windows computer user but as with anything, the more you use them the more comfortable with them you shall be.

THE "COMMAND" KEY

1) The key that you will most often use will be the "command" key which is on either side of the spacebar.

This key will have *either* an symbol on it **or** the word "command" **and** the "Bowen Knot" symbol:

The "command" key is used in a variety of *keyboard shortcuts* which will be explained and demonstrated throughout this book.

THE "CONTROL" KEY

2) The "control" key (bottom row of keyboard) is important as it enables you to "simulate" a right mouse click.

To get a *pop-up menu* to appear for example, you can *press and hold down* the "control" key as you click the mouse:

The Apple computer mouse is really the only major hardware difference (from a user viewpoint anyway) between Macs and PCs.

Once you get used to the idea that you need to hold down the "control" key while you are clicking the mouse to simulate a right mouse click, that hardware difference will become a non-issue.

THE "OPTION" KEY

3) The "option" key corresponds to the "alt" key on Windows computer keyboards.

The "option" key (located on the bottom row of the keyboard between the "command" key and the "control" key) is also used in a variety of keyboard shortcuts / commands.

The ⌥ symbol is used to indicate the "option" key.

THE "DELETE" KEY

The "delete" key on the upper right side of the keyboard has the same function as the "backspace" key on a Windows keyboard:

Pressing the "delete" key moves the "blinking line" (text insertion point) to the **left** (erasing any text unfortunate enough to be in its path).

You can press the *smaller* delete key (on a full-sized Apple keyboard) to erase text to the **right** of the "blinking line":

To simulate the "right" erasing delete key on an Apple *notebook* (or laptop) computer, you can press and hold down the "Function" key (fn) on the lower left corner of the keyboard while you are pressing the "delete" key:

THE "ARROW" KEYS

You can press the "Arrow" keys on the lower right side of your keyboard to scroll up and down web pages and windows:

You can also press the keyboard arrow keys to move the "blinking line" (text insertion point) around text area boxes, web address boxes, and text boxes on web forms.

Using the keyboard whenever possible instead of the mouse will both save you time and reduce wear and tear on your wrist that results from too much mouse use.

THE "RETURN" KEY

The "return" key on the middle right side of the Apple keyboard corresponds to the "Enter" key on a Windows computer keyboard and serves the same purposes.

You can for example, type a web address into the Safari web address box and then press the "return" key (one time) to visit that web site.

"Return"

If you can't type, check a "how to type" book out of your local library and practice the exercises in that typing book on your Apple computer keyboard.

The Mac Computer "Desktop"

The Mac computer desktop *looks* a bit different than the Windows desktop but it works pretty much the same way.

Mac Computer Desktop

The computer "desktop" is so named because it's very similar (at least conceptually) to the top of a regular desk.

The Mac computer desktop has three main components: the Program Dock, the "Finder" menu, and the Hard Disk icon.

THE "FINDER" MENUS

When the Finder program is **active**, you will see the "Finder" **menus** at the top left corner of your computer screen:

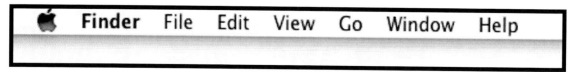

"Finder" is the brains of your Mac computer, it's the one program that will *always* be running.

It is not possible (thankfully!) to quit or close the Finder program as your Mac would be an attractive high-tech paper weight without it.

Finder Icon

Finder doesn't have a Windows counterpart but it's not a program that you have to think too much about.

You can click on a blank area of your Mac computer desktop to make Finder the "active" program.

You can use the "Finder" menus to do such things as:

1) Sort the files on your desktop (or the files in an open Finder window) by name, size, date, and kind:

2) Quickly access folders, locations, and utilities on your Mac *without* opening a window:

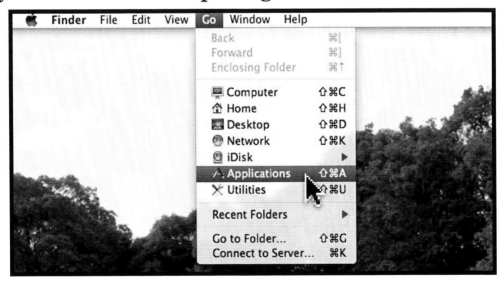

You can *switch* to the Finder program by using the mouse to single-click the "Finder" icon on the program dock.

Please note the keyboard shortcuts next to each menu selection on the Finder menus.

For example, if **Finder** is the active program, you can press the "shift", "command", and the "H" keys at the same to time to cause your Mac's "Home" folder to open.

THE HARD DISK ICON

The "hard disk" icon on your Mac computer desktop corresponds to the "My Computer" icon on the Windows computer desktop:

The hard disk icon on the Mac desktop is like a *doorway* into your Mac computer.

If you *double-click* the Hard Disk icon, a "Finder" window will open:

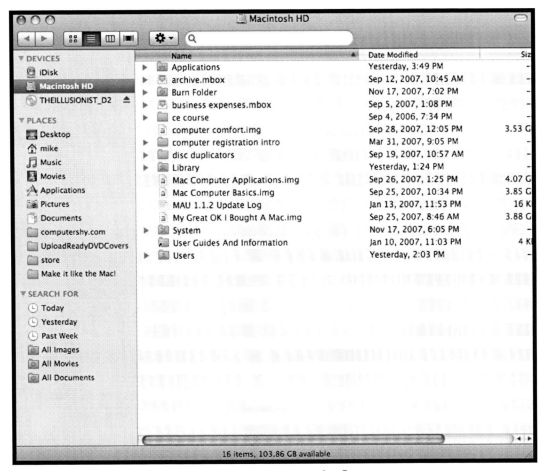

Mac Computer Window

You can use this Finder window to access all the **programs** and **files** on your Mac computer (we'll talk more about this window in the "Basic Operations" chapter).

THE PROGRAM DOCK

You can quickly start programs from the program dock by using the mouse to click *one time* on the icon of the program that you wish to start:

Tip of Screen Arrow over "Safari" Icon on the Program Dock

Like most everything else on your Mac computer, the program dock can be *customized*. You can add or remove shortcut icons from the program dock.

We talk about how to do this in the "How to customize your Mac" chapter.

 The video demonstrations for the preceding chapter are prefaced by "Desktop" at: http://gallery.mac.com/help4computershy ·

Mac Computer Basic Operations

- Shut Down, Restart, & "Sleep"
- How to start a program from the "dock"
- How to start a program from the "Applications" folder
- How to "quit" Mac programs
- How to empty your trash
- Mac "Windows"

SHUT DOWN, RESTART, & "SLEEP"

You can restart, shutdown, and put your Mac to "sleep" from the Menu.

The Apple menu corresponds to the "start" button on a Windows computer.

The Apple menu will *always* be at the top left corner of your computer screen regardless of which program is currently "active" on your Mac computer.

1) Use the mouse to place the tip of your screen arrow directly over the symbol at the top left corner of your Mac computer screen.

Hold the mouse very still and then click the mouse button one time.

This will cause a drop-down menu to appear:

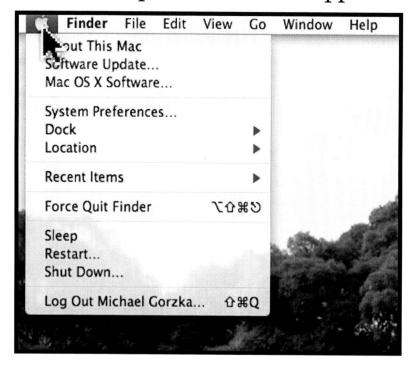

2) You can then use the mouse to select "Sleep" (an energy saving mode), "Restart", or "Shut Down":

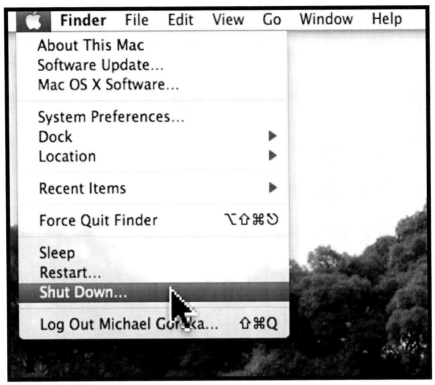

If you select "Restart" or "Shut Down", a window will appear asking if you *really* want to do this:

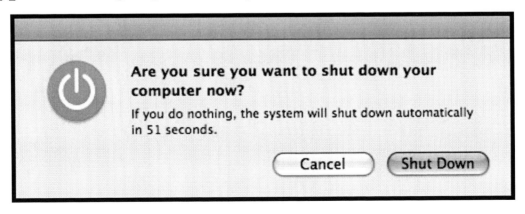

If so, you can simply press the "Return" key on the right side of your computer keyboard one time (or use the mouse to click the appropriate button).

Close or "Quit" any programs that you have open *before* you restart or shut down your Mac.

If you select the "Sleep" menu selection (by clicking it one time), your Mac will go into an *energy saving mode* (i.e. the computer screen will go black and your Mac will use less energy).

To wake your Mac back up again, press a key on your keyboard or click the mouse.

Apple recommends that you put your Mac to *sleep* instead of shutting it down unless you're going on vacation or something.

That being said, I have found that you do need to restart your Mac every so often (or do a complete shut down) even if you use your Mac every day.

You can also use the menu to access your System Preferences window, your program dock options, and to find out what your Mac computer has under the hood (i.e. "About this Mac").

If you ever have to contact Apple tech support, they're going to want the info from "About this Mac":

HOW TO START A PROGRAM FROM THE "DOCK"

By *default*, the program dock will be on the **bottom** of your Apple computer screen.

Your dock can be moved to different locations on your computer screen through the "Dock" selection on the menu.

However, if you are using Mac OS 10.5 ("Leopard"), you may want to leave your program dock on the bottom as it would look terrible anyplace else.

1) Use the mouse to place the tip of the screen arrow directly over the icon of the program that you wish to start:

Tip of Screen Arrow over "Address Book" icon on the Program Dock

2) Hold the mouse very still and then click the mouse *one time.*

The program should then start.

NOTE: You can choose to "hide" your program dock and cause the dock icons to *magnify* upon mouse over through the "Dock" submenu (which is located on the menu).

Single-click the program icons on the dock and *double-click* the program icons in the Applications folder.

HOW TO START A PROGRAM FROM THE APPLICATIONS FOLDER

If a program that you wish to use is *not* on your program dock, the next place to look is in the *Applications* folder.

You can *quickly* open your Mac's Applications folder by first making "Finder" the active program (by clicking on the Finder icon on your program dock or clicking on a blank area of your computer desktop) and by pressing the shift, command, and "A" keys all at the same time.

OR

1) Use the mouse to *double-click* (knock knock) the hard disk (drive) icon on your computer desktop:

Tip of Screen Arrow over the Hard Drive icon on the Computer Desktop

This will open a "Finder window" for you:

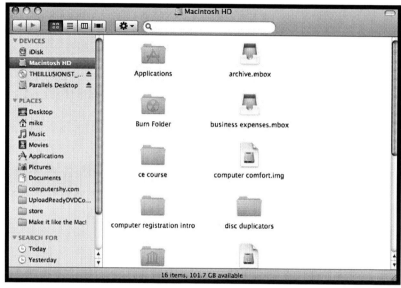

Mac Computer "Finder Window"

2) Use the mouse to click the "Applications" folder on the left side of the window one time:

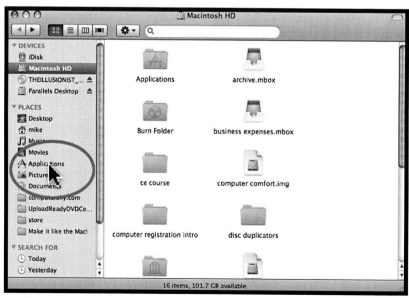

Tip of Screen Arrow over "Applications" Folder (circled)

This will open that folder in this window:

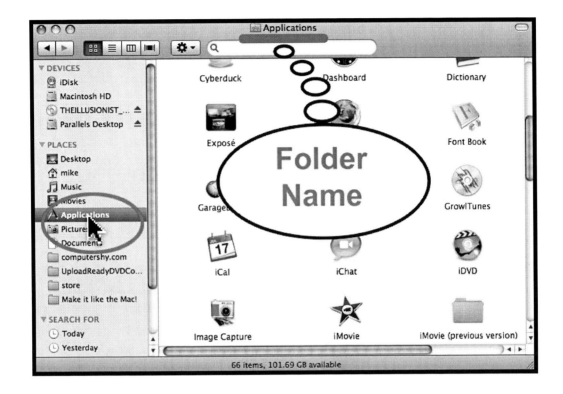

Once you have the Applications folder open, you have several options to find the program that you are looking for:

- You can scroll up and down the window until you see it.
- You can **sort** the contents of the folder using the "Finder" menu (View -> arrange) and *then scroll up and down the window.*
- You can type the name of the program that you are looking for into the window search box

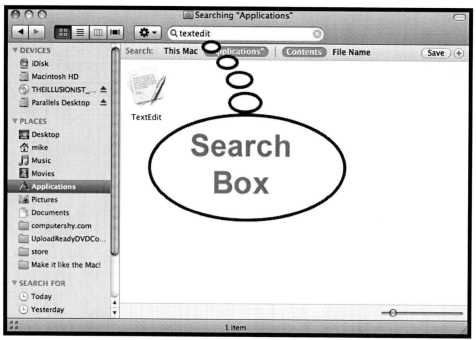

Program name typed into "Search" box

3) After you have found the program that you are looking for, use the mouse to "double-click" that program icon:

The program will then start.

 If you use a program quite often, it makes sense to put its shortcut icon on your program dock for easy access (see the online visual demonstrations).

HOW TO "QUIT" MAC PROGRAMS

1) You can quit a program by first clicking the program name at the top left corner of your computer screen.

2) Then use the mouse to select "Quit" from the drop-down menu:

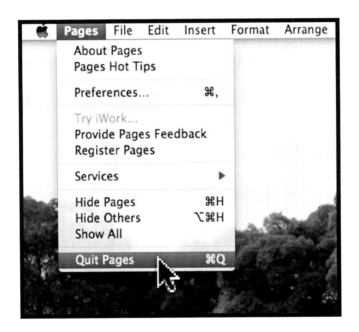

 To quit a program you can hold down one of the "command" keys (on either side of the keyboard spacebar) and then press the "q" key on time.

HOW TO EMPTY YOUR TRASH

You can follow this procedure to empty your Trash (which you should do periodically to conserve storage space on your Mac computer hard drive).

1) Use the mouse to place the tip of your screen arrow directly over the Trash can at the lower right corner of your Mac computer screen.

2) Hold the mouse very still --- and then press and *hold down* the mouse button until a small pop-up menu appears:

3) Use the mouse to click the "Empty Trash" menu selection.

If an alert window appears, use the mouse to click the appropriate button or simply press the "return" key on your computer keyboard to affirm that you do indeed wish to empty your trash.

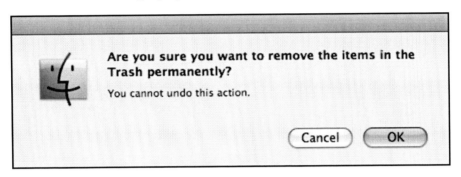

If "Finder" is the **active** program (i.e. if it says "Finder" at the top left corner of your computer screen), you can *simultaneously* press the "Option", "Shift", and "Delete" keys to empty your trash.

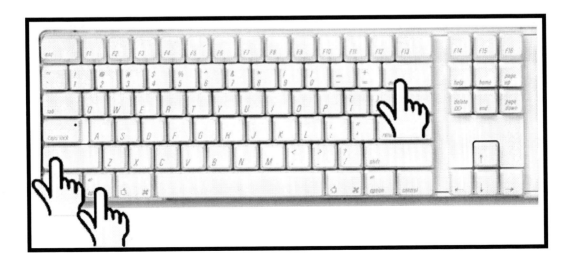

HOW TO OPEN A WINDOW

As stated earlier, a Mac computer window is a *doorway* to all the programs and files (documents, videos, songs, spreadsheets, photos, etc.) that are on your Mac computer.

To open a Mac computer window, you can double-click the hard disk icon as previously described.

You can *also* open a window by first switching to "Finder" and then by **holding down** one of the "command" keys on your keyboard and pressing the "n" key one time.

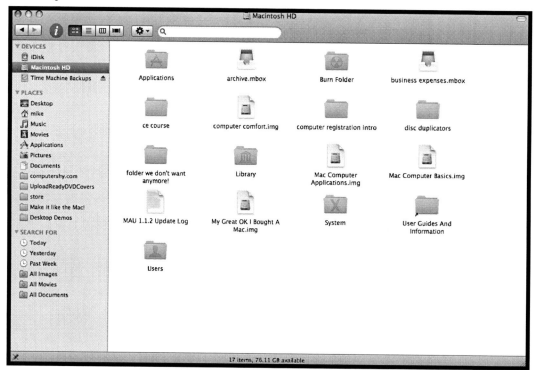

"Finder" Window

 Mac computer "windows" and Windows computer "windows" work pretty much the same way. Probably the biggest differences are the location of the buttons and where the window goes when it is *minimized*:

"Minimized" window next to Trash can

At the top left corner of most of the windows on your Mac computer you will find three buttons:

The red button at the far left is a **close** button, you can click this button to *close* an open window.

The orange button (center) is a **minimize** button, you can click this button to make the window very small (please see the online movies for a cool visual demo of the Minimize button in action).

You can "minimize" all of your open windows to reveal your computer desktop but a faster way to do that would be to press the "F11" key on your keyboard.

The **keyboard shortcut** to *minimize* an active window is to hold down the "command" key and press the "m" key one time.

NOTE: You can click a minimized window to enlarge it.

The **green** button to the right of the Minimize button is the *resize* button. You can click that button to **resize** the window.

The visual demonstrations for this chapter are prefaced by "Basic Ops" at http://gallery.mac.com/ help4computershy

How to set up Email on Your Mac

- Get your email account info (from your ISP or Help for the Computer Shy)
- Start the Mail program
- Fill out the Email setup screens

GET YOUR EMAIL ACCOUNT INFO

The *first* thing that you need to do to set up the Apple Mail program to send and receive email messages is to get your email account information.

If you have your own Internet Service Provider, you can call them and ask them for the following information:

- Your Email Address

- Your Email Password

- Your "Account Type" (which will probably be POP)

- Your "Incoming Mail Server"

- Your "Outgoing Mail Server"

If you would like a "computer shy" email account, please contact your favorite stalwart and intrepid computer help company at: www.computershy.com/contact.

START THE APPLE MAIL PROGRAM

Start the *Apple Mail* program by using the mouse to single-click the "Mail" icon on your program dock:

FILL OUT THE EMAIL SETUP SCREENS

The first time you start the *Mail* program on your new Mac, an email account setup window will probably appear prompting you for your email account information.

If the email account setup window does *not* automatically appear….

1) Use the mouse to click "Mail" at the top left corner of your computer screen:

2) Select "Preferences" from the drop-down menu:

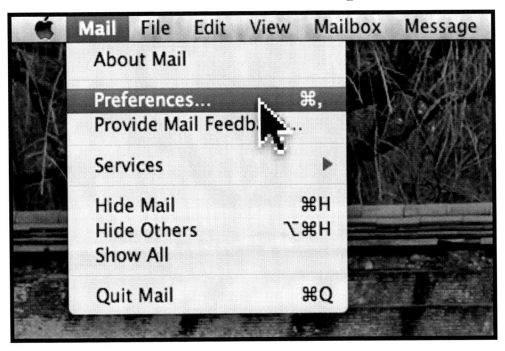

This will cause the Mail "Preferences" window to appear.

You can hold down one of the "command" keys on the bottom row of your keyboard and then press the comma key (,) to get the "Preferences" window for the program on your Mac that you are currently using (i.e. the "active" program).

preferences window keyboard shortcut

3) Use the mouse to click the "Accounts" tab at the top of the preferences window:

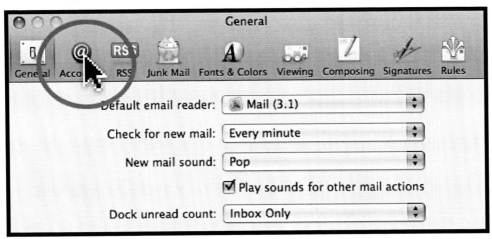

This will open the "Accounts" screen in the window:

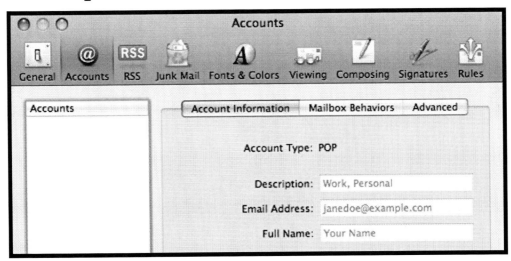

NOTE: you can look at the top of the window to see which section of the preferences window that you are currently in.

4) Click the plus sign (+) at the lower left corner of the window:

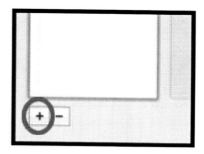

This will cause an "Add Account" screen to appear.

5) *Carefully* type in the required information on this screen and then press the "Continue" button at the lower right corner of the window.

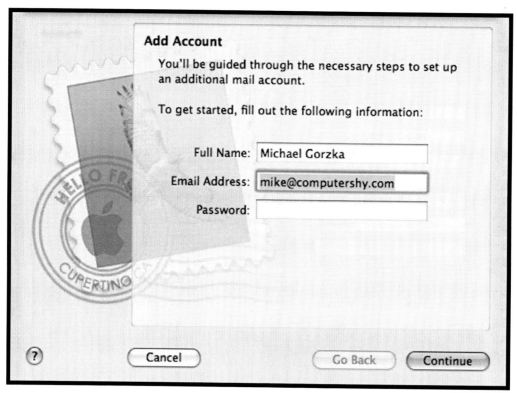

Complete each of the setup screens the same way.

Please don't try to rush through this procedure (as I have so many times before).

Slow and steady *definitely* wins the race here!

It's also worth mentioning that your Mac must be connected to the Internet in order for this procedure to work.

The Mail set up procedure will take about 5 minutes or so depending on your Internet connection and email service provider.

You will then be able to send & receive email messages on your Mac!

File Management

- TextEdit Demo (save as .rtf, .doc)
- How to create folders
- How to move files from one folder to another
- How to delete a file or folder
- How to find a file (Spotlight)
- How to rescue a file from the trash
- How to get "info" on a file or folder
- How to set a file to be opened by a specific program
- Common file extensions

In this chapter, we're going to create a file with the *TextEdit* word processing program and then perform various file management actions on it.

TEXTEDIT DEMO

 *TextEdit* is a word processing program that comes bundled with Mac computers. It works very much like Microsoft Word and can in fact, open documents that were created with Microsoft Office 2007.

TextEdit doesn't have as many features as Microsoft Word but it does fulfill a lot of Word Processing needs.

TextEdit

How to Create a Document

By default, the *TextEdit* icon is **not** on your program dock so we'll have to start *TextEdit* from within the Applications folder as described in the "Basic Operations" chapter in this book:

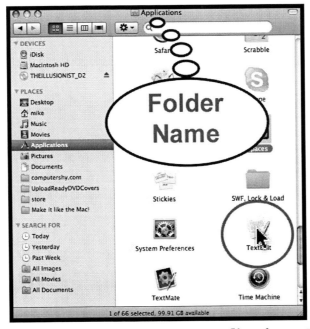

TextEdit Icon (circled) in the Applications Folder

After the TextEdit program has been started, you can start typing just as you would with the Microsoft Word or WordPad program:

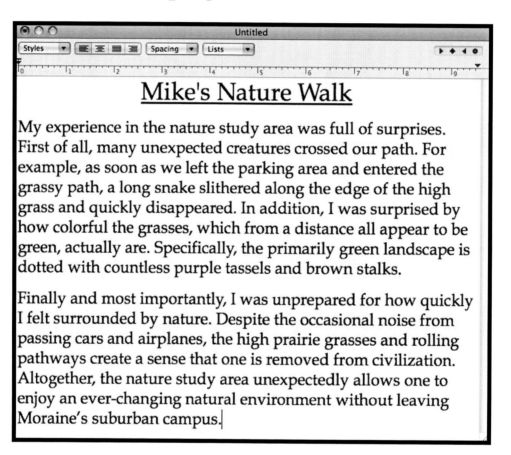

 You can instantly *hide* all other open programs (**except** the program that you are currently using) by pressing the "option", "command" and the letter "h" keys all at the same time.

How to Save a Document

 The "Save" procedure on a Mac is very much the same as the procedure to save a document on a Windows computer (the "Save" windows will look a bit different but that's about it).

You will have to **name** the document you are saving and select a **location** on your Mac to save it to.

1) You can use the mouse to select "Save" from the TextEdit "File" menu *or* you can simply hold down a "command" key and press the "S" key one time:

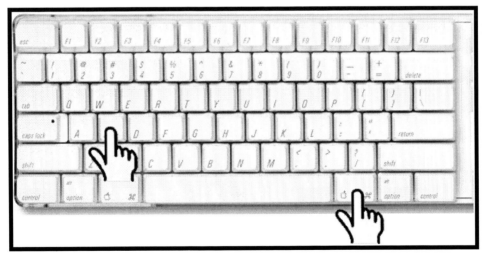

CMD + S Keyboard Combination

As with a Windows PC, the **first time** you save a document, a "Save As" window will appear:

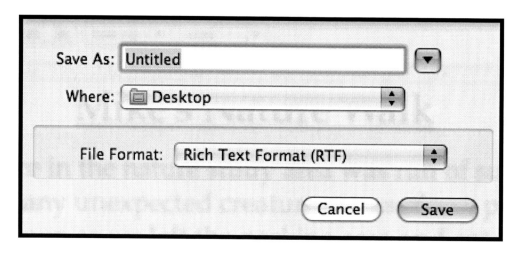

Please note in the above picture that the word "Untitled" is *highlighted*.

2) This means that you can type in a more descriptive file name for your document *without* having to click inside that box first:

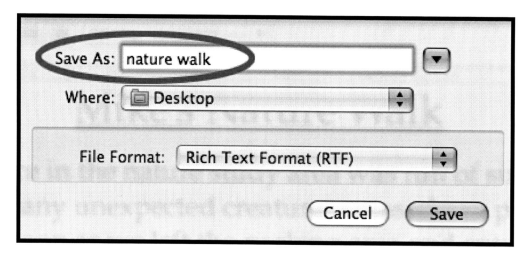

3) After you type a name for your document in the "Save As" box, you can click on the "Where" box one time:

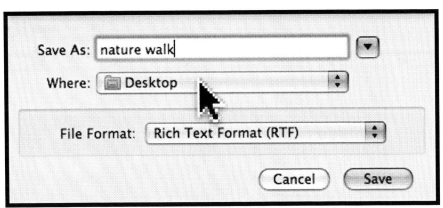

4) Select a **location** on your Mac from the drop down menu to save this document in:

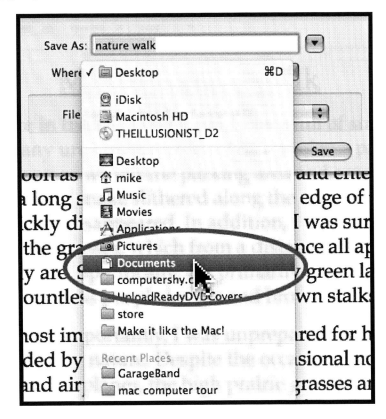

Next up on the "Save As" window, is the "File Format" box:

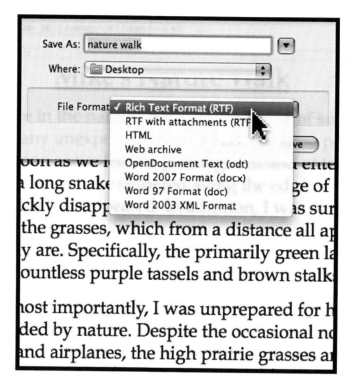

If you are going to be sending this document to a Windows computer user who has Microsoft Office 2007 installed on their computer, you can select the "Word 2007" format:

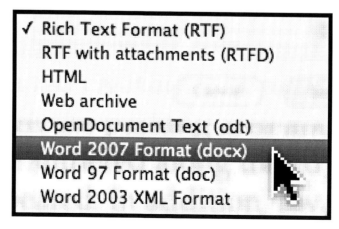

If you are not sure *which version* of Microsoft Word your Windows-using compadre has (& you wish to retain the **formatting** of your document), you can select *Rich Text Format* (RTF) from the File Format menu.

Just about any word processing program on God's still somewhat green earth can open an RTF document.

After you have *named* your document; selected a *location* on your Mac computer for it to reside in; and selected a *File Format* for it; you can click the "Save" button **or** simply press the "Return" key on your keyboard one time.

We take a more in-depth look at the TextEdit program in the *Mac Computer Applications* instructional DVD available at www.computershy.com

HOW TO CREATE FOLDERS

Here is the document that we just created in the "Documents" folder:

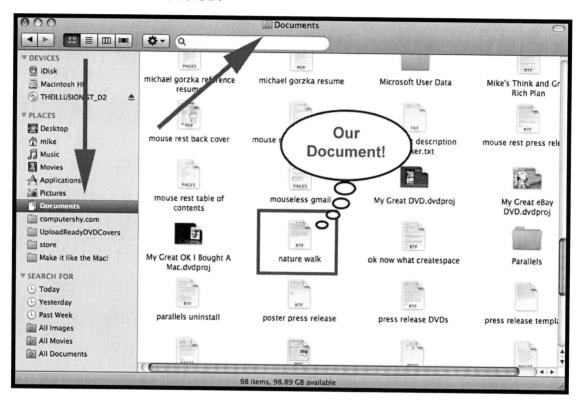

For the sake of organization, I usually save my various letters, book chapters, essays, and other literary musings in the "Documents" folder on my Mac.

Please see the "Basic Operations" chapter for a review on how to find items in folders.

Let's say that we want to create a *sub-folder* within the "Documents" folder for the document that we just created (& for other essays on the same subject).

There's a couple of ways you can do this.

1) You could select "New Folder" from Finder's *File* menu:

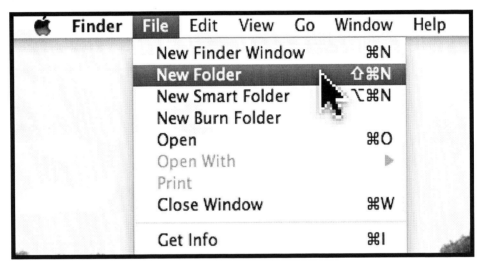

NOTE: If you don't see "Finder" at the top left corner of your computer screen, you can click the "Finder" icon at the *far left* corner of your program dock.

2) Or you could press the "Shift", "command", and the "n" keys all at the same time.

This will cause a **new folder** to appear in the window that we are currently in (in this example the "Documents" folder window):

Please note in the above picture that the words "untitled folder" are *highlighted*.

This means that we can immediately type in a descriptive name for this newly created folder:

HOW TO MOVE FILES FROM ONE FOLDER TO ANOTHER

Now that we have created and named a new folder, we want to *move* the file that we created from its present location (the "Documents" folder) to its new home (i.e. the "Nature Essays" folder we just created *within* the Documents folder).

There are several ways we can accomplish this.

One way is to *drag* and *drop* the file:

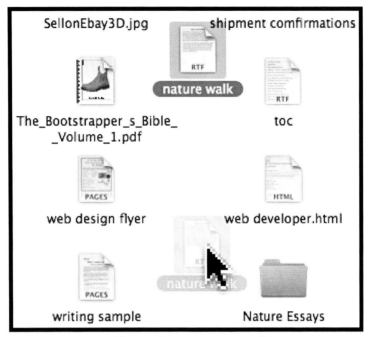

File Being "Dragged"

Files can be "dragged and dropped" the same way on a Mac as they can be "dragged and dropped" on a Windows computer.

Place the tip of the screen arrow over the file that you wish to drag and drop. *Hold down* the mouse button and the move the mouse on the mousepad in the direction that you wish to "drag" the file.

When the file is *directly* over the location that you wish to drop it into; stop moving the mouse on the mousepad and release the mouse button that you had been holding down.

Another way to **move a file** is to first *copy* the file that you wish to move and then *paste* it in another location or folder.

First use the mouse to place the *tip* of your screen arrow directly over the file that you wish to move:

nature walk

Hold down the "control" key on the bottom row of your computer keyboard:

And then click the mouse one time.

This will cause a "pop-up" menu to appear.

Release the "control" key that you had been holding down and use the mouse to select the "copy" menu selection:

Double-Click the folder that you wish to move the file into:

This will *open* that folder:

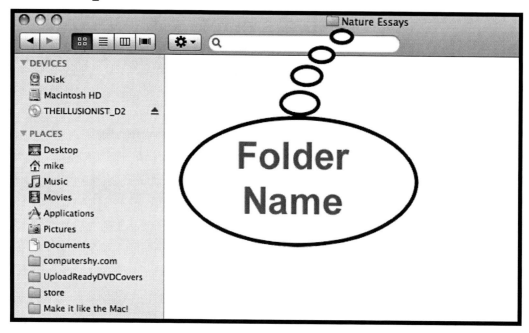

Hold down one of the "command" keys on your keyboard and press the "v" key one time:

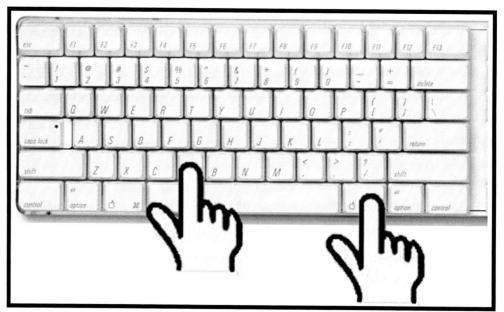

"command + v" Keyboard Combination

This will *paste* the file you copied into that folder:

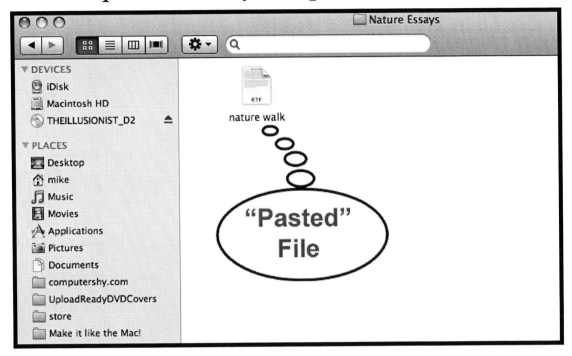

HOW TO DELETE A FILE OR FOLDER

In this section we're going to **delete** the file in the *Documents* folder that we just **copied** and pasted into the "Nature Essays" folder.

1) Use the mouse to click the item to be discarded **one time** (*double-clicking* on a file or folder will open it).

This will *highlight* that file:

2) Press and *hold down* one of the "command" keys on your keyboard and then press the "delete" key one time:

"command + delete" keyboard combination

This will send that file to your Mac computer Trash (located at the lower right corner of your computer screen).

HOW TO FIND A FILE

If you ever forget where you saved a file, you can use the "Spotlight" program to find it.

In this example, we're going to use *Spotlight* to find the "Nature Walk" document that we created in the first section of this chapter (& then moved to a different folder).

The great thing about *Spotlight* is that you don't have to remember what you named a file or where you saved it.

If you can remember words in the title or *anywhere* in the document, you can use Spotlight to find it.

To invoke *Spotlight*, you can click the "magnifying glass" icon at the top right corner of your Mac's computer screen:

You can then type in some words that you know are in the document that you are looking for:

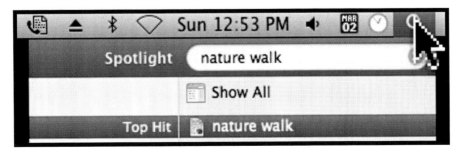

1) You can also press the "option", "command" and the "spacebar" keys at the same time.

This will cause a Spotlight search window to appear:

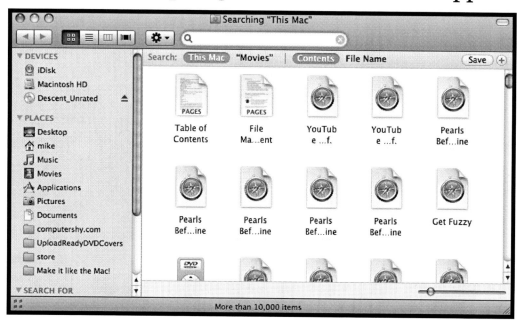

2) Type some words that you know are in the file that you are looking for into the **search box** at the top of the window:

3) Look in the Spotlight window for the file that you are looking for:

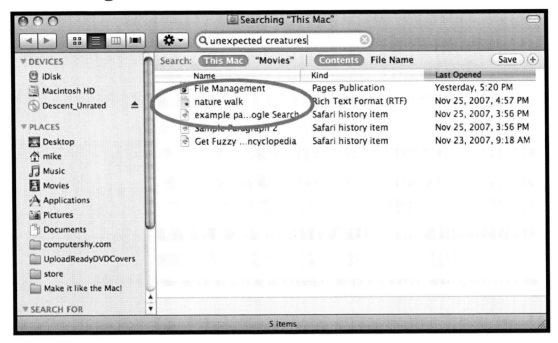

4) Use the mouse to *double-click* that file:

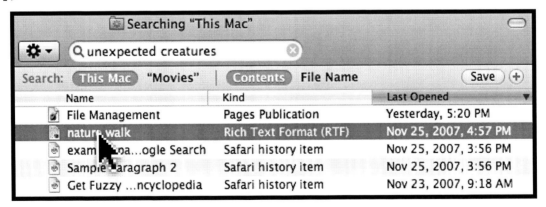

The file should then open.

HOW TO RESCUE A FILE FROM THE TRASH

You can retrieve any files from the Trash that you have deleted *as long as you haven't emptied your trash yet.*

 Windows computers have a "Recycle Bin" on the computer desktop. Mac computers have a "Trash Can" at the lower right corner of the desktop.

1) Use the mouse to place the tip of your screen arrow directly over the trash can at the lower right corner of your Mac computer desktop.

2) Hold the mouse very still and click the mouse one time.

This will open your Mac computer Trash folder.

3) Look around the Trash folder for the file or folder that you want back:

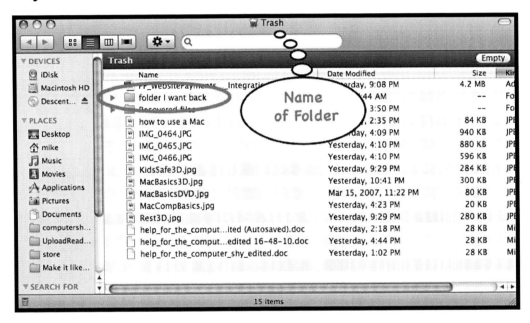

4) Use the mouse to place the tip of the screen arrow directly over the file or folder that you want to rescue from the Trash and then *press and hold down* the mouse button:

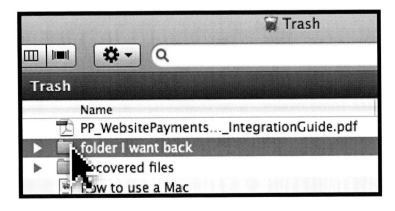

5) As you are *holding down* the mouse button, move the mouse on the mousepad to *drag* the file out of the Trash folder:

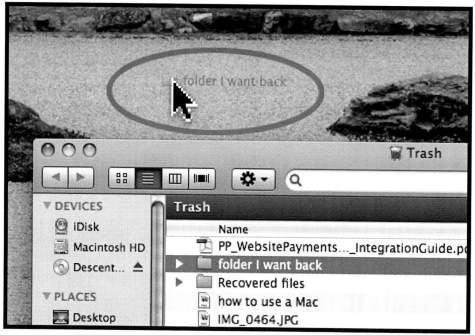

File being dragged clear of the Trash folder (circled)

6) When the file is *clear* of the Trash folder, stop moving the mouse on the mousepad and release the mouse button that you had been holding down.

NOTE: You can also "copy and paste" files using the method described in the previous section to rescue items from your Trash folder.

This will put that rescued file on your computer desktop:

You can then "copy & paste" or "drag & drop" the file to a different folder or location on your Mac as previously described:

Video Demonstrations for the various File Management topics that we cover in this chapter can be found at http://gallery.mac.com/help4computershy

HOW TO GET "INFO" ON A FILE OR FOLDER

To get *information* on a file (such as the file's size and when it was created), you can first *hold down* the "control" key on your keyboard and then click the file one one time.

Select "Get Info" from the "pop-up" menu:

 A *quicker* way to get a file's info is to click on the file one time; **hold down** the "command key"; and then press the "I" key one time.

Either of these actions will cause an "information" window to appear which will tell you the size of the file, its location on your Mac hard drive, and when it was created, modified, & last opened.

"Info" Window

HOW TO *SET* A FILE TO BE OPENED BY A SPECIFIC PROGRAM

You can use the "Info" window to open a file (and other files like it) with a particular program.

For example, I currently have *two* PDF readers on my Mac: "Adobe Reader" and "Skim".

Presently, if I double-click a PDF icon, Adobe Reader will launch and display that PDF Document for me.

But let's say that I want "Skim" to be the *default program* to open PDF files on my Mac. Here's how we can make the switch...

1) Bring up the "Info" window for the file as previously described.

2) Click the "Open with" box one time:

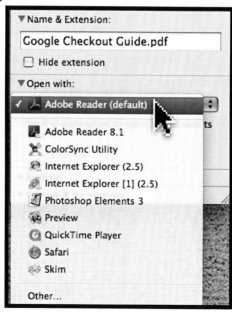

3) If the program that you wish to open that file with is in the *list of programs* that appears, you can click that program one time:

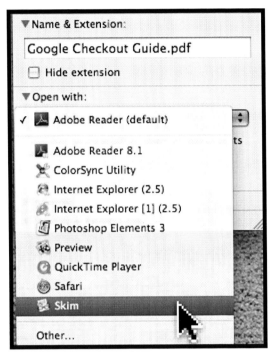

You can then click the "Change All" button to open all the other files on your Mac that have the same file extension (.pdf in this example) with the program that you just selected:

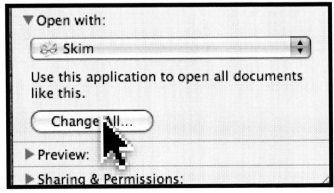

COMMON FILE EXTENSIONS

.pdf (portable document format) - easily shared between Windows and Mac computers.

.txt (plain text) - easily shared between Windows and Mac computers.

.doc (Microsoft Word) - can be opened with the "TextEdit" program on your Mac.

.mov (quicktime video format) - can be opened on Windows computers with the "Quicktime for Windows" program.

.ppt (Microsoft PowerPoint) - can be opened with "Keynote" which is part of Apple's *iWork* software package which is **not** part of the Mac's included software bundle and must be purchased separately.

.xls (Microsoft Excel) - can be opened with the Numbers program (also part of Apple's *iWork* software package).

.mp4 (audio & video files) - cannot be opened on a Windows computer without special software.

How to Transfer Files from a PC to Your Mac

WINDOWS vs. MAC COMPATIBILITY

As we shall see in the next section, moving files from your Windows PC to your new Mac is a very simple procedure.

You may have to download or purchase additional software for your Mac (especially for business applications) but by and large, compatibility between Macs and PCs is no longer much of an issue.

 If you have any compatibility issues, please email me at mike@computershy.com before purchasing any additional software.

Some files (at least without additional software) will be "Windows" only. Your Mac will not be able to open them or even understand what they are.

First the good news!

Files from your Windows computer that your Mac will welcome with open arms:

- Text documents (.txt)
- Microsoft Word documents (.doc)
- Microsoft Excel spreadsheets (.xls)
- Microsoft PowerPoint presentations (.ppt)
- Photos (.jpg)
- Graphics (.gif, .tif, .png)
- Portable Document Format files (.pdf)

You can exchange music files between Macs and PCs but only from Windows iTunes to Mac iTunes.

HOW YOU CAN TRANSFER YOUR DATA FROM YOUR WINDOWS COMPUTER TO YOUR NEW MAC

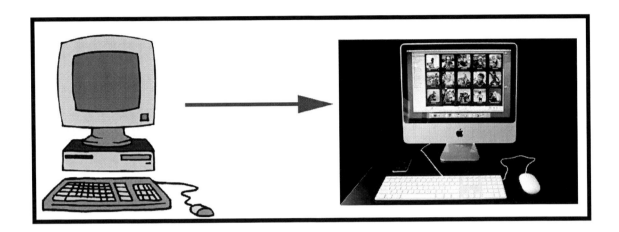

There are numerous ways you can move the files on your PC to their new Mac home. Here are three of them:

1) If you have an Apple Retail Store in your area, you can use their "PC Data Transfer Service" to move your files from your moldy oldy PC to your shiny new Mac.

2) You can "burn" your Windows files onto a CD or DVD and then copy the files from that CD or DVD onto your new Mac.

3) You can also *copy* your Windows files to a USB external hard drive (or a *Firewire* hard drive if your

PC has a firewire port) such as the LaCie 500 GB
Brick:

 Firewire ports have this symbol next
them:

USB ports are designated by this symbol:

 You should buy a 500 GB external hard
drive anyway. They've gotten to be pretty
cheap and the "Time Machine" program
in Mac OS 10.5 makes scheduled data
backups a snap!

http://www.youtube.com/watch?v=XnDz1Q4ck6c

There are two ways you can copy files and folders from your PC to the external hard drive (without any special software):

1) "Drag & Drop"

2) "Copy & Paste"

To make your Windows to Mac file transfer easier, you can copy entire folders (such as the "My Documents" folder) from your Windows computer to your external hard drive.

1) To *copy* a file or folder from your Windows computer to the external hard dive, first click *one time* on the file or folder that you wish to copy:

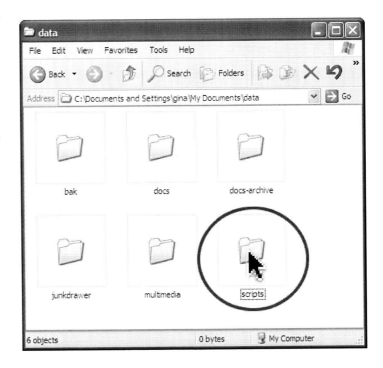

2) Hold down one of the "control" keys on your Windows keyboard and press the "c" key one time:

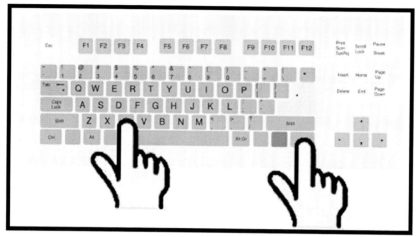

This will **copy** that folder (and everything *in* that folder) to the invisible clipboard on your Windows computer.

3) Double-click the "My Computer" icon on your Windows computer desktop and then double-click the external hard drive icon:

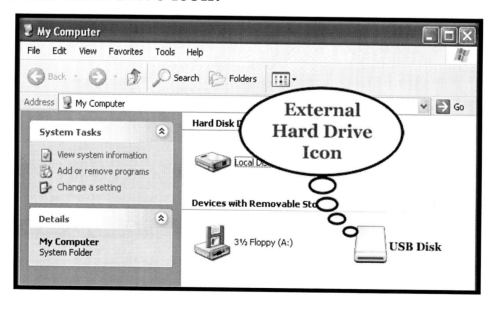

4) After you have opened the external hard drive window, you can hold down the "control" key on your Windows keyboard and press the "v" key one time:

This will *paste* the folder that you copied from your PC to the external hard drive.

After you have finished copying and pasting your important files from your Windows computer to your external hard drive...

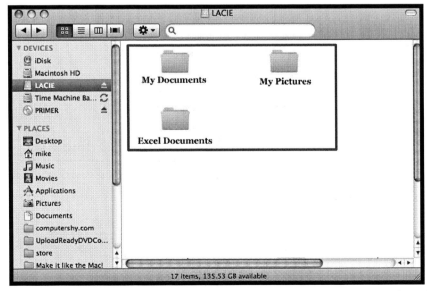

Folders From Windows Computer on External Hard Drive

You can then attach the external hard drive to your new Mac and then "drag & drop" (or copy & paste) the files from the external hard drive into the appropriate folders on your Mac (i.e. documents in the "Documents" folder, pictures in the "Pictures" folder, etc.)

External Hard Drive Attached to Mac Computer

To make your data transfer faster, you can *select all* the files in a particular folder on your external hard drive by holding down a "command" key on your Apple keyboard and pressing the "a" key one time.

After you have **selected** the files that you wish to move from the external hard drive to your new Mac, you can then drag them (or copy & paste them) as a *group* to the folder on your Mac Computer where you want them to be.

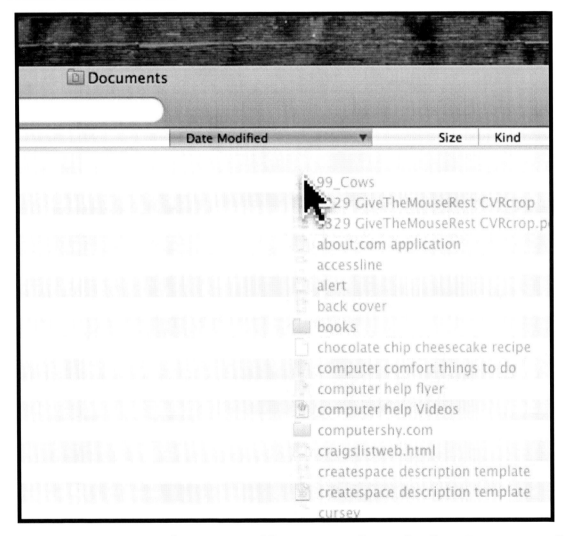

Files Being "Dragged & Dropped" en Masse from the "My Documents" folder on the External Hard Drive to the "Documents" folder on the Mac

PROCEDURE TO COPY & PASTE FILES FROM YOUR EXTERNAL HARD DRIVE TO YOUR MAC

1) *Select* the files that you wish to copy.

2) *Copy* the files to the invisible clipboard (both Macs & PCs have an "invisible clipboard").

3) *Open* the folder on your Mac that you wish to *paste* the copied files into.

4) *Paste* the files that you copied from the external hard drive.

The keyboard command to *copy* something on a Mac computer is "command + c" (i.e. hold down one of the "command" keys and press the letter 'c' key one time).

The keyboard command to *paste* something that you've copied to the clipboard is "command + v" (i.e. hold down one of the "command" keys and press the 'v' key one time).

The procedure really just comes down to this: Copy & Paste files from your PC to an external hard drive; Copy & Paste files from the external hard drive to your new Mac.

HOW TO OPEN YOUR IMPORTED WINDOWS FILES ON YOUR MAC

A "file" is *anything* that you can store on your computer (pictures, documents, spreadsheets, songs, videos, etc.)

It's worth repeating that **basic procedures** on Mac computers *are very much the same* as they are on Windows Computers.

You can open a file on a Mac computer the same way you would on a Windows computer.

1) Use the mouse to place the tip of the screen arrow directly over the file that you wish to open:

2) Hold the mouse very still and then double-click the Apple Mouse button (Knock Knock!).

If the Mac operating system understands what the file is (and chances are that it will if the file is a text document, a graphic, or a photo), it will choose the appropriate program on your Mac to open the file.

Your Mac will probably use the *TextEdit* program to open Microsoft Word Documents, for example.

Your Mac will use the *Numbers* program to open Microsoft Excel Spreadsheets (if *Numbers* is installed on your Mac).

Your Mac will probably use the *Preview* program to open photos and pictures.

If you want to select a *different* program to open a particular file, you can:

1) Hold down the "control" key on the bottom left corner of your Apple keyboard.

2) Click the file icon one time (& then release the "control" key that you had been holding down).

3) This will cause a *pop-up* menu to appear:

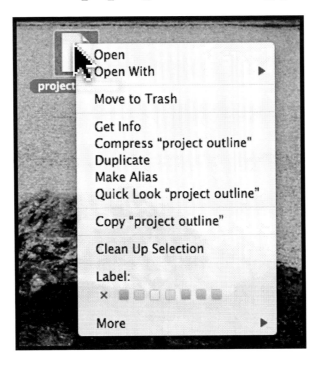

4) Place the tip of your screen arrow over the "Open With" menu selection:

5) *Click* the program that you want to open the file with on the "Open With" *sub-menu:*

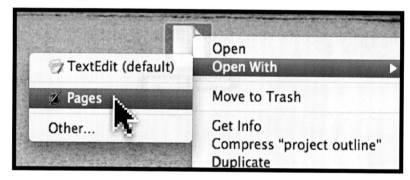

If you don't have to swap files back and forth between Windows computers then you probably won't have to do this very often.

If you *do* have to share files with a Windows computer (between home and office for example) then this procedure will become second nature very quickly.

ADDITIONAL MAC SOFTWARE

You may have to purchase additional software for your Mac to work with some of your Windows computer files (such as Microsoft Excel spreadsheets).

The most popular office applications for the Mac are *Microsoft Office for the Mac* and *Apple iWork 08*.

You can can use the iWork *Keynote* program to work with Powerpoint files; the iWork *Numbers* program to work with Excel spreadsheets; & the iWork *Pages* program to work with Word documents.

How to run "Windows" on Your Mac

Newer Mac computers (those made after January 2006) have *Intel* chips.

This means that you can (if you must) run the Windows Operating System (and Windows programs) on your Mac computer.

The three most popular methods for running Windows on a Mac computer are (at the time of this writing):

1. "Boot Camp" - a free Apple computer program which comes pre-installed on newer (2006 or later) Mac computers.
2. "Parallels" - a 3rd party program ($79.99) that enables you to switch back and forth between Windows and Mac operating systems *without* having to reboot your Mac computer.
3. Fusion - another 3rd party program ($79.99) which also enables you to run the Mac OS and Windows.

Fusion and Parallels have fully functional trial versions.

 Regardless of which way you choose to run Windows on your Mac, you will need to purchase your own copy of Windows.

These three programs enable you to install Windows XP or Windows Vista on a **partitioned area** of your Mac computer hard drive.

 The really good news here is that you don't have to get your hands dirty partitioning your Mac hard drive. The program that you choose will take care of that for you.

 The "Windows" side of your Mac computer *will be just as vulnerable* to **viruses** and **spyware** as a typical PC would be.

NOTE: If you want to run Windows Vista on your Mac, you need to purchase Windows Vista Business or Windows Vista Ultimate (The "Home" version of Vista will not work at the time of this writing).

BOOT CAMP

"Boot Camp" is included with newer Mac computers. It was created by Apple to enable you to run Windows on your Mac if you choose to do so.

To run the Boot Camp program...

1) Get an **unregistered** copy of the Windows program that you wish to install on your Mac (I got mine very cheap on eBay).

2) Double-click the "Boot Camp Assistant" icon which will be in the "Utilities" folder within your "Applications" folder:

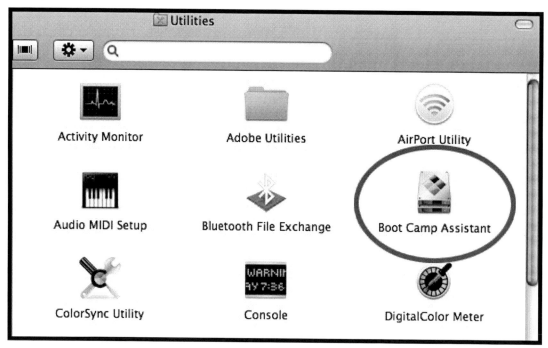

3) Carefully follow the onscreen instructions:

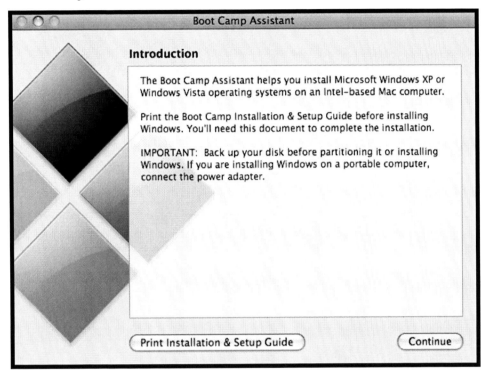

 If you use Boot Camp to run Windows on your Mac, you will have to **reboot** your Mac whenever you wish to *switch* between the Mac operating System and the Windows operating system.

PARALLELS DESKTOP FOR MAC

"Parallels Desktop for Mac" is a 3rd party software program that enables you to both install Windows XP (or Windows Vista) on your Mac and to run both the

Windows and Mac operating systems *at the same time.*

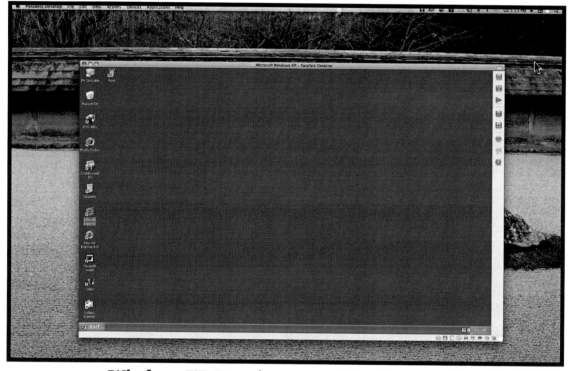

Windows XP Running on my Mac Computer!

The set up procedure for installing Parallels (and your preferred version of Windows) on your Mac is about as easy as it gets.

1) Download the *latest* version of "Parallels Desktop for Mac" from www.parallels.com.

2) Get your Windows installation CD ready (& its product registration key).

3) Double-click the "Install Parallels Desktop" icon:

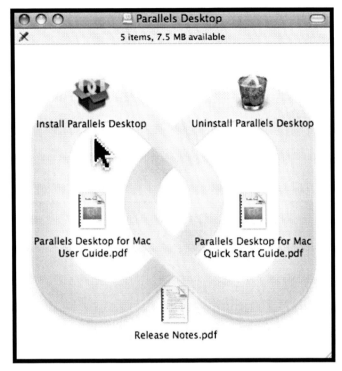

4) Follow the on screen instructions:

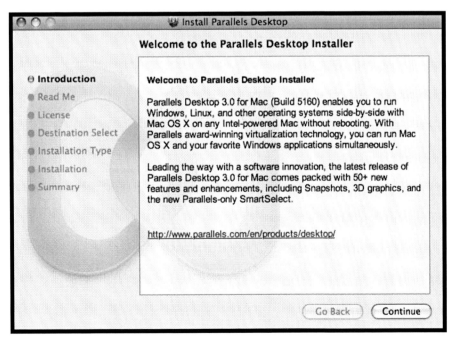

How To Start Parallels (and Windows)

Once you've installed *Parallels* onto your Mac computer, you can start the program (and start the Windows Operating System) just as you would any other program on your Mac.

By default, Parallels will **not** be on your program dock so you'll have to open it from the *Applications* folder.

TIP: Once Parallels has been started you can "control-click" its icon on the program dock to permanently add it to your program dock.

First we need to make *Finder* the **active** program.

To make Finder the active program you can click the "Finder" icon on the far left corner of your program dock:

Now that Finder is the **active** program, there are several ways you can open your Applications folder.

One way to open the Applications folder is to first open a "Finder window" by *double-clicking* the hard drive icon on your computer desktop:

After a "Finder window" has been opened, you can click "Applications" on the left side (navigation area) of the window:

 You can also open the Applications folder (when *Finder* is the active program) by simultaneously pressing the command, shift, and "a" keys.

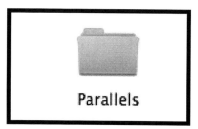

If you are a "menus" person, you can also select "Applications" from the Finder "Go" Menu.

After you have opened your Applications folder, look for the Parallels folder (which will be *within* the Applications folder):

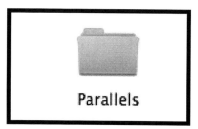

Parallels

Double-click this folder to open it and then double-click the "Parallels" icon:

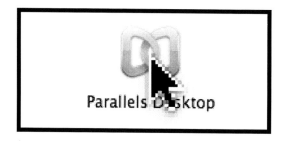

Parallels Desktop

This will start the "Parallels" program and whichever version of Microsoft Windows that you installed along with it.

After Parallels has been started, you can use your Mac just as if it were a Windows PC:

Everything will work just the same (with one minor exception).

To perform a *right mouse click* in the Windows environment, you'll need to **hold down** both the control and shift keys as you click the mouse.

Parallels (and the Windows operating system) will "run" inside a **window** just like any other program on your Mac.

This window (like any other window on your Mac) can be *minimized*, *resized*, and *closed* by clicking the buttons at the top left corner of the Parallels window:

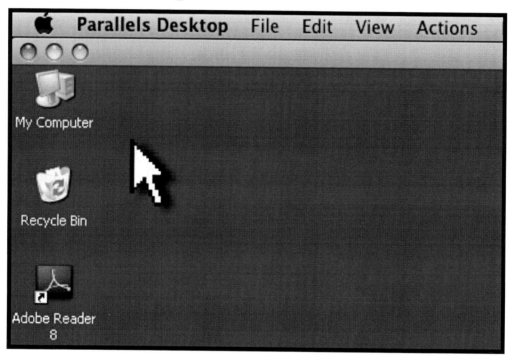

 To overcome the few remaining compatibility issues between Macs and Windows, you can **copy** files between the two operating systems by using the *copy & paste* methods as described in the "File Management" chapter of this book.

To switch from your Windows Operating system to your Mac OS (and vice versa) you can **hold down** the "command" key on your keyboard and press the "tab" key:

The "command" + "tab" keyboard command enables you to *toggle* between open applications on your Mac.

You can hold down the "command" key and keep pressing the "tab" key until the application that you wish to switch to is selected (as "Finder" is in the above picture).

You can **shut down** the Windows environment on your Mac by clicking the "Shut Down" button on the Windows "Start Menu" (just as you would normally shut down a PC).

Since Parallels is really another program on your Mac, you can "quit" Parallels (and shut down the Windows operating system on your Mac) by selecting "Quit" from the Parallels menu:

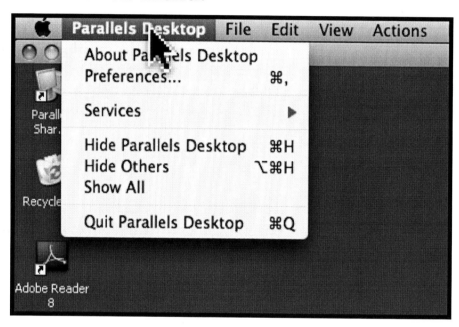

Even though Parallels is a program on your Mac, you should still treat the "Windows" section of your Mac *as if it is an actual PC.*

You should turn your Windows firewall on; practice "safe computing"; and install virus protection software.

You can install software on the Windows environment of your Mac just as you would on an actual PC (by either downloading the *necessary software* from the Internet or installing it from a CD).

How to *Customize* Your Mac Computer

- Desktop picture & screen saver
- Screen saver
- Program dock tricks
- Desktop icons

HOW TO CHANGE YOUR DESKTOP PICTURE

1) Use the mouse to click the "Apple" () at the top left corner of your computer screen and select "System Preferences" from the drop-down menu:

This will cause the "System Preferences" window to appear.

2) Use the mouse to click the "Desktop & Screen Saver" tab one time:

This will cause the *Desktop & Screen Saver* preferences window to appear.

3) If necessary, use the mouse to click the "Desktop" tab near the top of this window:

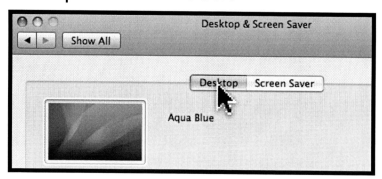

On the left side of the window you will see some picture folders.

4) You can click on any of these folders to display the pictures in that folder on the right side of the window:

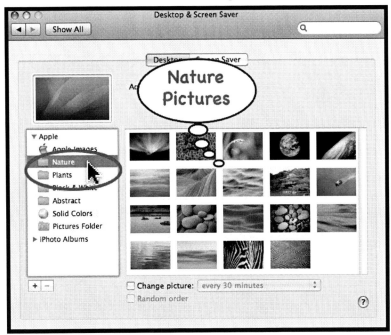

5) To *select* one of these pictures for your Mac computer Desktop, simply click the picture one time:

HOW TO SELECT A SCREEN SAVER

1) Follow the previous procedure to access the "Desktop & Screen Saver" preferences window.

2) Click the "Screen Saver" tab near the top of the window:

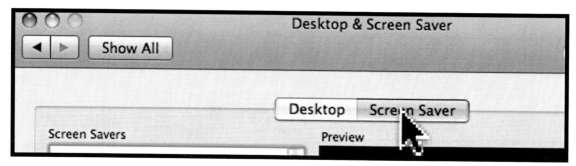

On the left side of the **Screen Saver window** will be a selection of Screen Savers.

3) Use the mouse to select the Screen Saver that you would like to use (such as "Word of the Day"):

A *preview* of that screen saver will appear on the right side of the window:

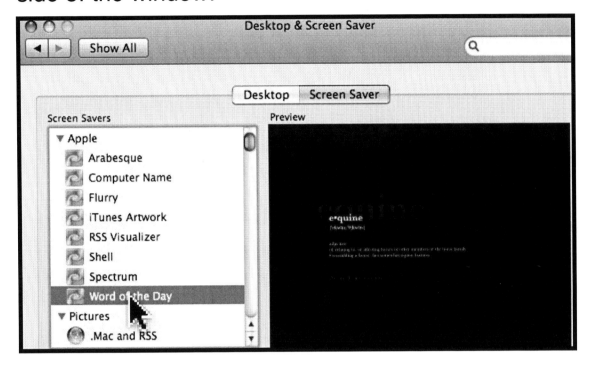

Near the bottom right corner of the window you will find an "Options" button that you can click to *modify* the screen saver; a "Test" button that you can click to preview the screen saver at full size; and a timer to *start* the screen saver:

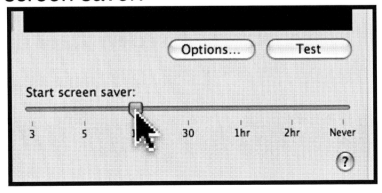

DESKTOP OPTIONS

Program Dock

As previously discussed, your Program Dock will be at the **bottom** of your Mac computer screen:

By default, the program dock will always be visible. If you find this distracting or if you would like some more screen real estate, you can first click the at the top left corner of your computer screen:

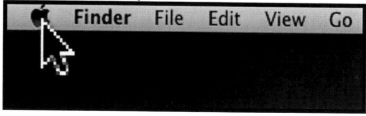

Then use the mouse to select *Dock* from the drop-down menu.

This will cause a "sub-menu" to appear.

Use the mouse to select the *Turn Hiding On* menu selection:

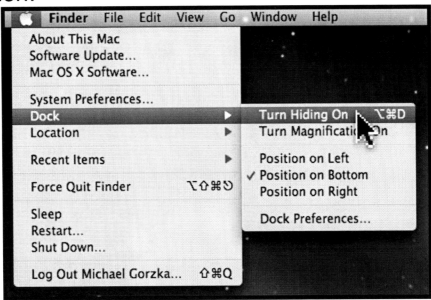

Now the program dock will be **hidden** from view. To see the program dock again, use the mouse to place the tip of your screen arrow at the bottom of your computer screen:

This will cause the dock to "pop up".

You can also select "Turn Magnification On" from the Dock submenu to get this effect:

Hide the Desktop Icons

Some of the desktop pictures will be so pretty that you will not want any of the desktop icons to block the view!

You don't have to display them if you don't want to.

These storage locations (hidden icons or not) will still be accessible from the Finder window *navigation menu* (on the left side of window).

Use the mouse to select the "Preferences" menu selection from the "Finder" menu:

This will cause the "Finder Preferences" window to appear.

When Finder is the active program, you can hold down the "command" key and press the comma key (,) one time to cause the Finder preferences window to appear.

Use the mouse to select *which* icons you would like to appear on your computer desktop:

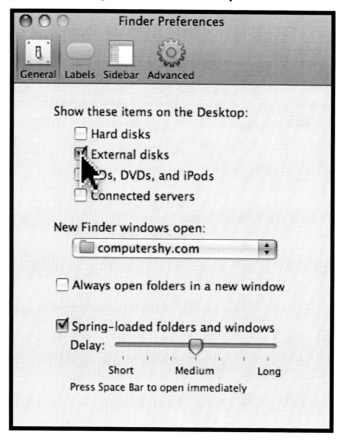

And then use the mouse to **close** the "Finder Preferences" window by clicking the red close button at the top left corner of the window:

 You can **close** any open window by holding down the "command" key and pressing the "w" key one time.

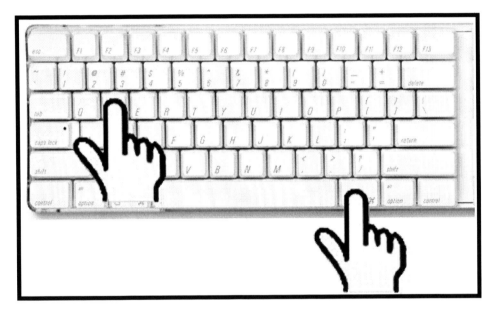

 Can I still open a "Finder" window if I hide the Hard Disk icon?

 Yes, you can. Hold down the "command" key on your keyboard and press the "N" key one time.

This will open a "Finder" window for you:

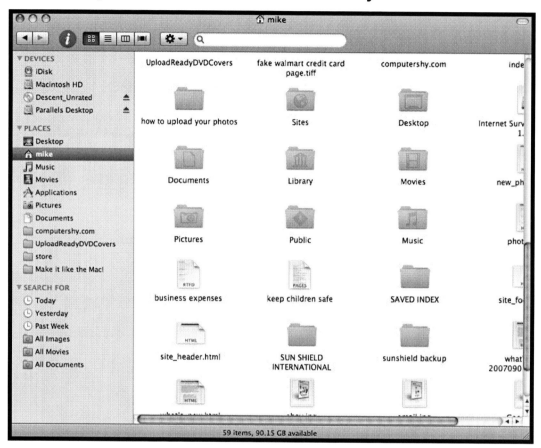

The "Finder" window is like a doorway into your Mac computer. You can access **all** of your Mac's programs and **all** of your files that you have stored on your Mac from the Finder window.

HOW TO ADD A PROGRAM ICON TO YOUR PROGRAM DOCK

To add a program icon to your program dock, start the program from the Applications folder as previously described.

This will put a "temporary" icon for that program on your program dock.

Place the tip your screen arrow directly over that temporary icon:

Hold down one of the control keys on your computer keyboard and click the mouse one time.

This will cause a pop-up menu to appear.

Release the control key that you had been holding down and select the "Keep in Dock" menu selection:

The icon will then remain on your program dock after you quit the program.

HOW TO REMOVE A PROGRAM ICON FROM YOUR PROGRAM DOCK

To remove an icon from your program dock, place the tip of the screen arrow directly over the icon that you wish to remove from the program dock.

Hold down the "control" key and click the mouse one time.

Select "Remove from Dock":

The visual demonstrations for this chapter are prefaced by "customize" at http://gallery.mac.com/help4computershy

Spotlight on "Spotlight"

Apple's "Spotlight" program provides a great way to find your wayward files!

Spotlight Icon

If you know *part* of a file name or if you know some words that are *in* a file, you can use "Spotlight" to quickly find it for you.

In this demonstration, I'm going to use Spotlight to find a recipe for Chocolate Chip Cheesecake that I know is *somewhere* on my Mac computer.

1) First use the mouse to click the Spotlight icon at the top right corner of the computer screen:

2) Type what you are looking for into the Spotlight search box.

For example, I can't remember what I named the document that has the recipe that I'm looking for but I remember the word "Oreo" is in it:

As soon as you start typing into the Spotlight search box, a list of search results will appear.

The second search result (circled) is the one that I'm looking for:

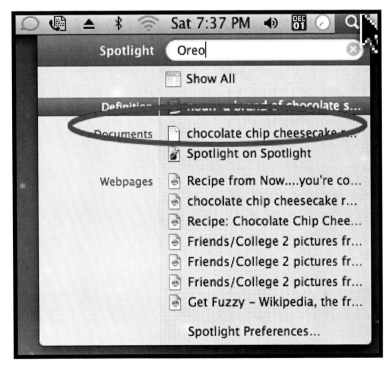

To *open* a file in a Spotlight search results list, simply use the mouse to double-click it:

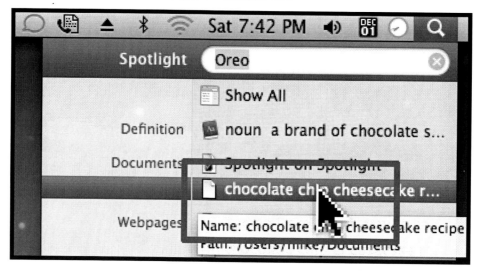

This will open that file for you:

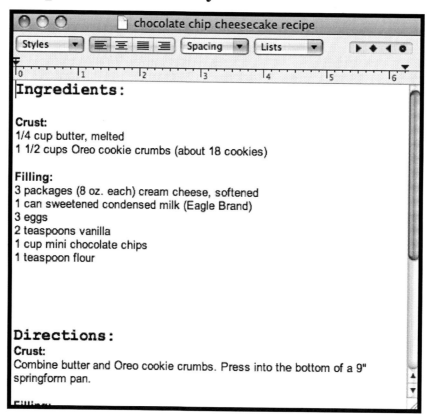

 Instead of clicking the Spotlight icon, you can press the "option", "command", and the "spacebar" *all at the same time*:

option + command + spacebar

This will cause a Spotlight *window* to appear which will work the same way as the Spotlight Search box:

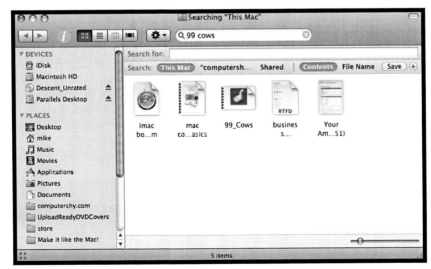

Apple Mail 101

- How to start Apple Mail
- How to open an email message
- How to reply to an email message
- How to compose a new email message
- Apple Mail keyboard shortcuts
- Email pictures
- How to attach pictures to email messages
- How to delete email messages
- How to "rescue" email messages from the trash
- How to "quit" the Apple Mail Program

HOW TO START APPLE MAIL

First use the mouse to start the Apple Mail program by clicking its icon on the program dock one time:

The Apple Mail program will then start.

HOW TO OPEN AN EMAIL MESSAGE

To open an email message in the Apple Mail program, use the mouse to *double-click* the email that you wish to open:

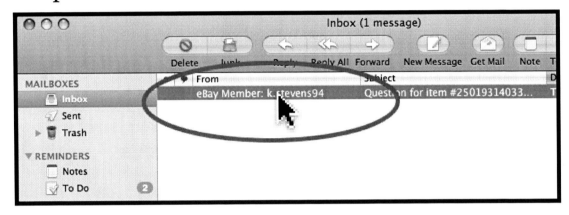

This will open that email message for you to read:

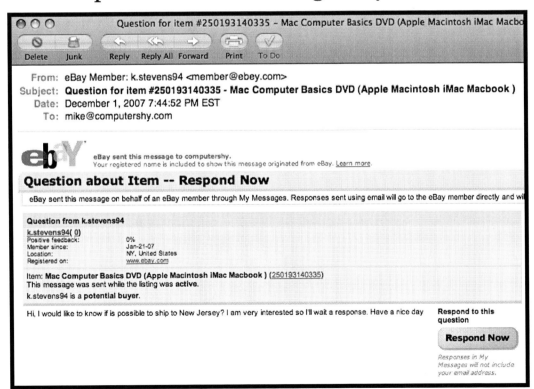

By the way, I need to point out here that this email message that I'm using for an example is a scam!

Please note that it says "ebey" instead of "ebay":

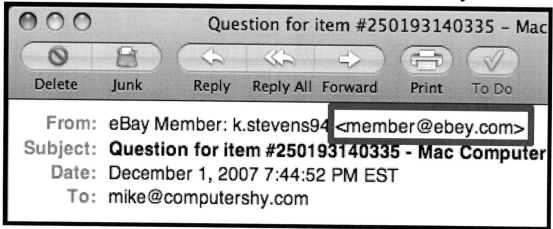

From: eBay Member: k.stevens94 <member@ebey.com>
Subject: **Question for item #250193140335 - Mac Computer**
Date: December 1, 2007 7:44:52 PM EST
To: mike@computershy.com

Unfortunately, there are a lot of cyber-no-goodniks out there who are looking to scam people! It definitely pays to be careful.

HOW TO REPLY TO AN EMAIL MESSAGE

First *open* the email message that you wish to reply to and then click the "Reply" button near the top of the email message window:

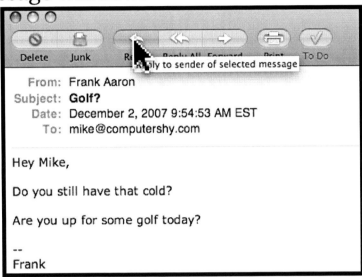

This will cause a Reply screen to appear:

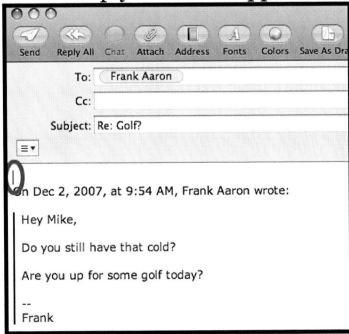

As with any Windows email programs that you have used, the person's email address will already be in the "To:" box and the "blinking line" (text insertion point) will already be in the email message box (circled in the previous picture).

So all you have to do is to type your email message reply into the email message box and then click the "Send" button at the top of the email message window:

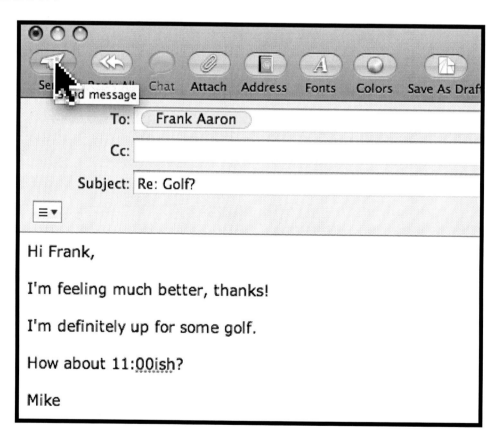

Does the Apple Mail program have a built-in spell checker?

Yes, it does. TextEdit, Safari, and Apple Mail all use the same spell check program.

To spell check a document, a text box, or an email message, press the "command", the "shift", and the "colon" keys all at the same time:

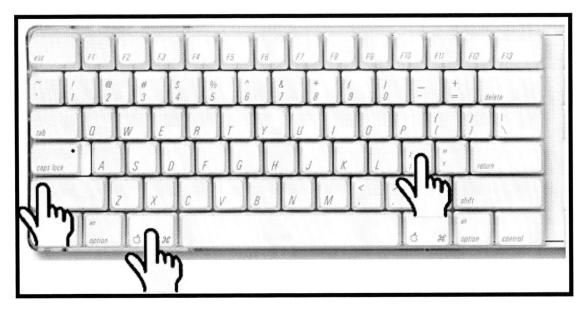

This will cause the "Spelling and Grammar" window to appear:

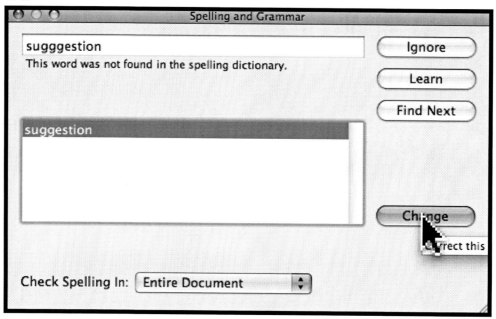

The Spell Checker is pretty straightforward. A possible misspelled word will appear in the box at the top of the window.

You can select one of the suggested spellings from the list that appears in the box below that and then click the "Change" button.

If the word is *not* misspelled, you can click the **Ignore** or the **Learn** buttons:

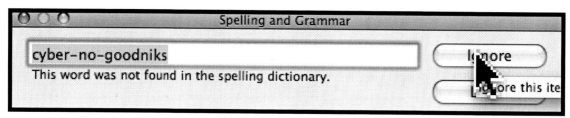

HOW TO COMPOSE A NEW EMAIL MESSAGE

1) Use the mouse to click the "New Message" button at the top of the **Mail** window:

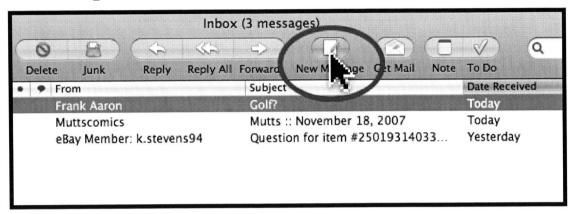

This will cause a "New Message" window to appear:

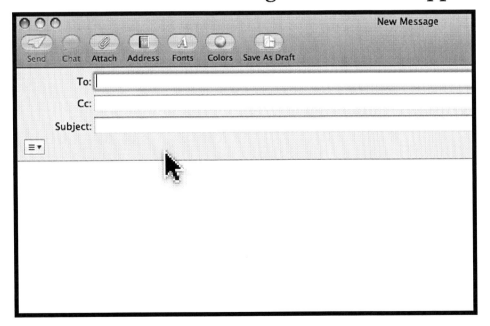

NOTE: By default, the "blinking line" (text insertion point) will be in the **To:** box.

 There's nothing especially new here for experienced Windows users but here's a brief rundown on how to send an email message using Apple Mail.

1. Type the email address of the person that you are writing to in the **To** box.

2. Type a brief subject for your email message in the "Subject" box.

3. Type your email message in the message box.

4. Click the "Send" button at the top of the "New Message" window:

APPLE MAIL KEYBOARD SHORTCUTS

- *Send* an Email message: "command" + "shift" + "d"
- *Reply* to an Email message: "command" + "r"
- *Close* an email message window: "command" + "w"
- *Open* an email message: "command" + "o"
- *Print* an email message: "command" + "p"
- Empty email trash: "command" + "k"
- Erase Junk Email: "option" + "command" + "j"
- Quit Apple Mail: "command" + "q"
- Get new mail: "command" + "shift" + "n"
- Open a new email message window: "command" + "n"

EMAIL PICTURES

If someone emails you a picture, Apple Mail gives you several options:

- Save it to your hard drive

- Print it

- Take a "Quick Look" at it

- Add the picture to iPhoto

How to Save an Email Picture to Your Hard Drive

1) Use the mouse to **press** (not *click*) the "Save" button near the top of the message window.

This will cause a short menu to appear:

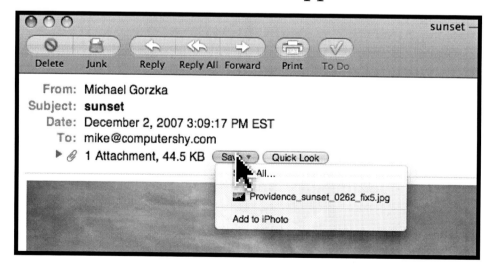

2) Use the mouse to *select* the picture that you wish to **save** on this menu:

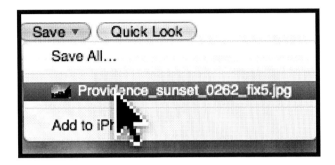

This will cause a "Save As" window to appear:

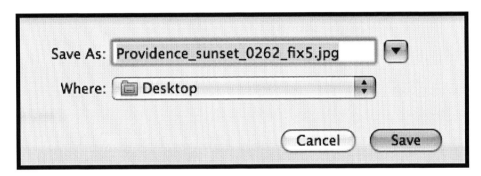

3) You can (if you wish) type a new *file name* for the picture in the "Save As:" box.

4) Select a *location* on your Mac by using the mouse to click the "Where" box one time and then by selecting a location on your Mac computer hard drive (such as the "Pictures" folder) to save the picture in.

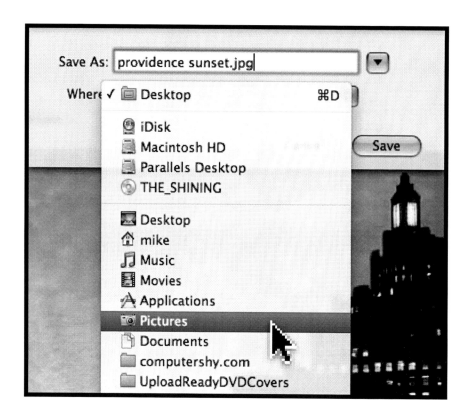

4) Finally click the "Save" button one time (or press the "Return" key on your computer keyboard):

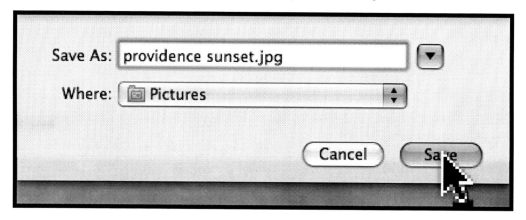

How to Save an Email Picture to iPhoto

You can easily add a photo (or a graphic) to your iPhoto library by instead selecting "iPhoto" from the *Save* menu:

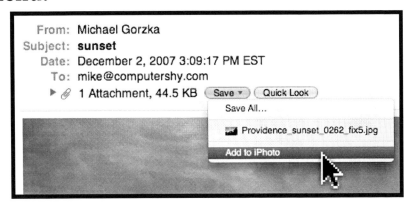

How to get a "Quick Look" at an Email Picture

A nice new feature in the *Leopard* (Mac OS 10.5) version of Apple Mail is the "Quick Look" button.

You can click the "Quick Look" button to see a full size version of the picture:

How to Print an Email Picture

This feature is pretty self-explanatory. You can click the "Print" button to send the email message (and the attached picture) to your printer:

It's worth repeating that this will send not only the attached picture to the printer but also the text of the email message itself.

If you want to print *only* the picture, you can:

1) Download (i.e. "save") the picture / photo to your Mac hard drive.

2) Navigate to the folder that you saved the picture to (or use "Spotlight" to find the picture) and *double-click* that picture's icon.

3) Print the picture from the program that opens it (which will be "Preview" by default) by selecting "Print" from that program's **File** menu.

Please note the keyboard shortcuts next to each menu selection:

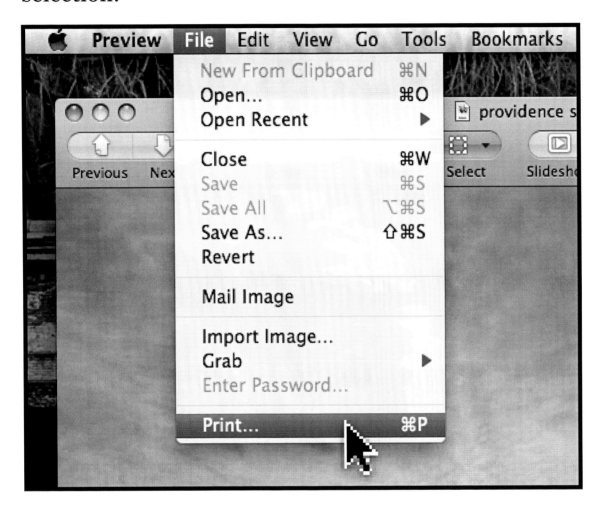

 The *default* program to open images on your new Mac will be "Preview" but as described in the *Basic Operations* chapter, you can "set" your default picture editor to be a different program.

HOW TO ATTACH PICTURES TO EMAIL MESSAGES

1) Compose a new email message as previously described:

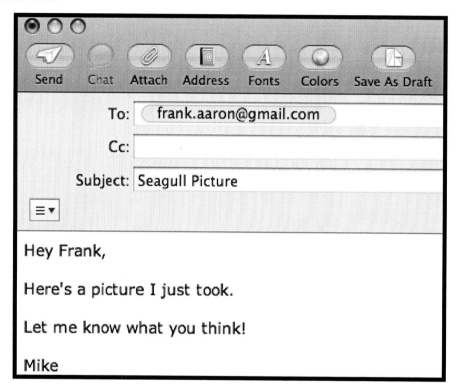

2) Use the mouse to click the "Attach" button near the top of the "New Message" window:

This will cause a "Choose File" window to appear.

You'll use this window to *navigate* to the folder on your Mac computer hard drive where the picture is that you wish to attach to this email message.

NOTE: This window may look a bit different than its Windows counterpart but it operates just the same.

3) Use the *navigation menu* on the **left side** of the window to select the folder that the picture is in:

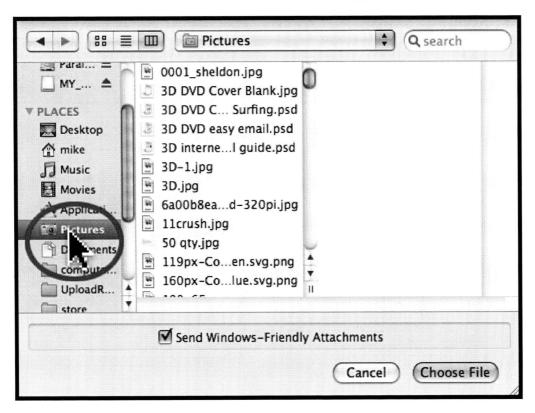

4) This will display the *contents* of that folder in the center column of the window:

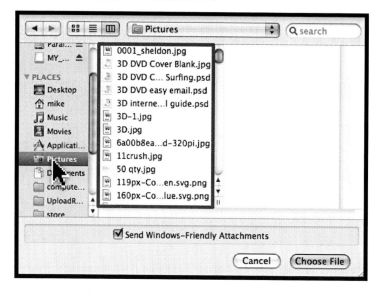

If necessary, *scroll* down the center column by using the scroll bar on the right side of the column.

5) *Select* the picture that you wish to attach to the email message by clicking that picture one time:

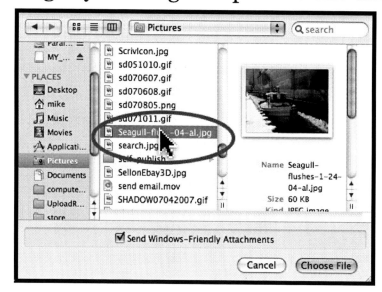

6) Click the "Choose File" button at the lower right corner of the window:

This will *attach* the picture to the email message:

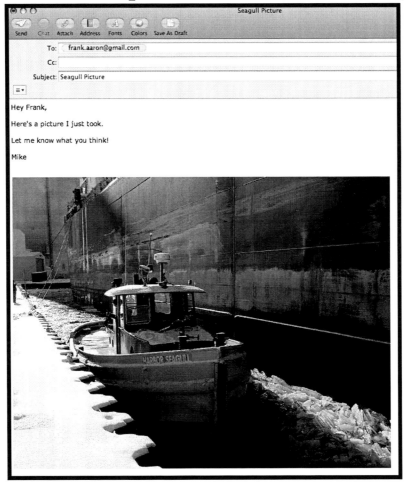

7) The only thing left to do now is to click the "Send" button.

HOW TO DELETE EMAIL MESSAGES

To delete an email message from your **Mail** Inbox (i.e. send it to the email Trash), first use the mouse to click *one time* on the email message that you wish to delete:

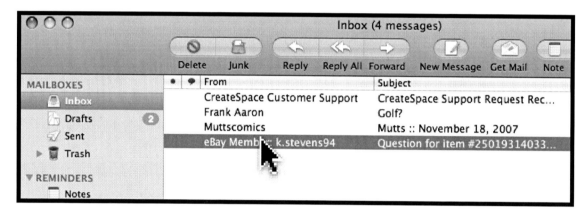

Then you can either use the mouse to click the "Delete" button at the top of the **Mail** window or press the "Delete" key on your keyboard one time:

HOW TO "RESCUE" EMAIL MESSAGES FROM THE TRASH

If you ever delete an email message by mistake (or need it back in your Inbox for whatever reason), you can *rescue* it from your email Trash.

This procedure will only work if you have **not** emptied your trash since the message was deleted.

1) First click the *Trash* folder one time:

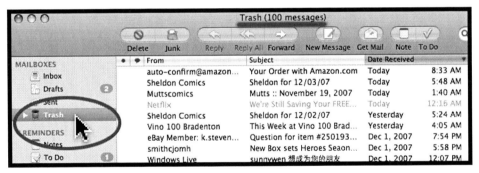

2) Click *one time* on the email that you wish to move back to your Inbox:

3) Press and *hold down* the mouse button.

4) As you are holding down the mouse button, move the mouse on the mousepad to *drag* the email message to your Inbox folder:

5) When the email message is directly over the **Inbox** folder, stop moving the mouse on the mousepad and release the mouse button that you had been holding down.

This will "drop" the email message into your Inbox.

You can "drag and drop" messages between other email folders as well.

6) You can return to your **Inbox** folder by clicking "Inbox" one time on the left side of the Mail window:

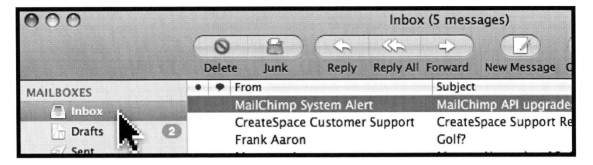

If you are using a notebook computer, instead of "dragging & dropping" the email, you may want to select "Move to Inbox" from the Message Menu:

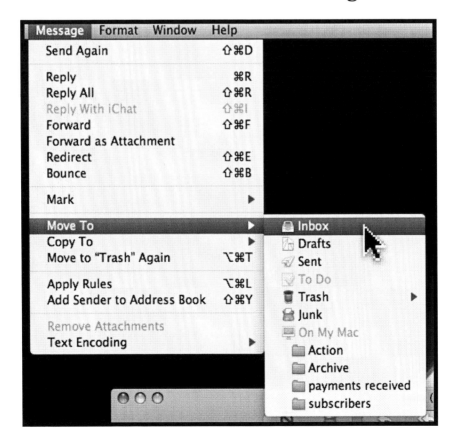

HOW TO EMPTY YOUR EMAIL TRASH

The quickest way to empty your email trash is to hold down the "command" key and press the "k" key one time:

A window will then appear asking if you *really* want to empty your email trash:

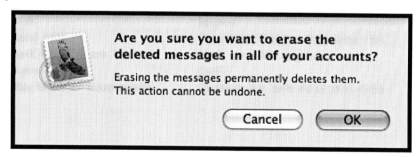

If you do wish to empty your email trash, simply press the "return" key on your Apple keyboard one time.

The "Are you sure" window will disappear and your email trash will empty

 Emptying your email trash will not necessarily erase the email messages from your email account. Contact your ISP or email provider for details.

HOW TO QUIT THE MAIL PROGRAM

You can close or "quit" the Apple Mail program by selecting the "Quit Mail" menu selection from the "Mail" menu:

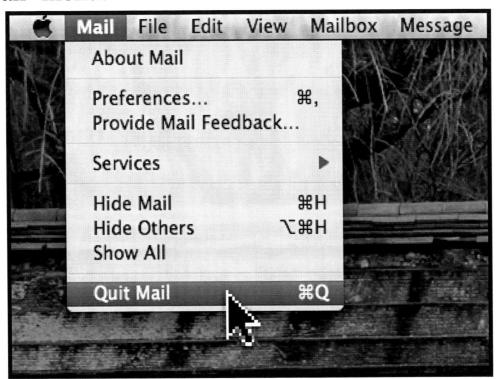

 You can also use the "command + q" keyboard shortcut (which you can use to close any of your Mac computer applications).

command + Q keyboard shortcut

 If you want to be instantly notified of new email messages, you can leave "Mail" open.

In my experience, you can leave **Mail** open as long as you are using your computer without it affecting your Mac's performance.

Incoming mail messages make a *sound* when they come in.

This sound can be set in the Mail preferences window:

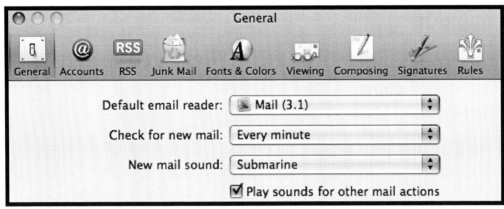

The number of *unread* messages that you currently have in your Inbox will appear on the "Mail" icon on the program dock.

The Apple Safari Web browser

If you have used Internet Explorer and /or Mozilla Firefox on a Widows computer, you're pretty much good to go with the Apple Safari Web browser.

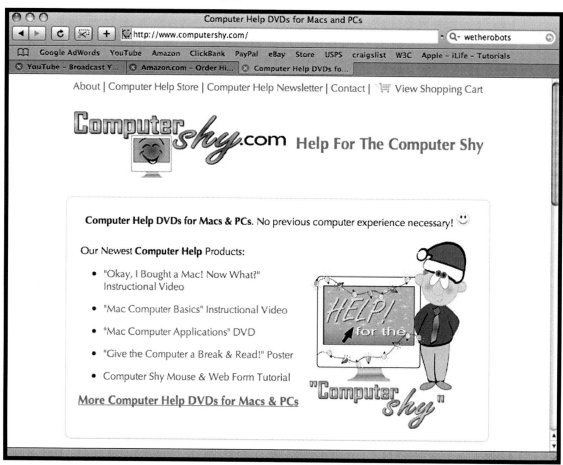

Web browsers are like cars in that they look different but do the same things and work pretty much the same way.

There's just a few things that we need to talk about here:

- How to use the Safari Web address box
- Safari "Tabs"
- Safari "Bookmarks"
- Google Search Box
- The "Back" Button

HOW TO USE THE SAFARI WEB ADDRESS BOX

As with IE or Firefox, you can use the Apple Safari Web address box to take you from one web site to another:

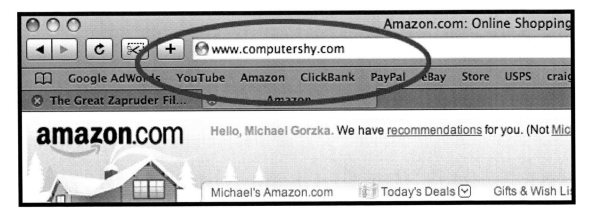

Assuming of course that you know the web address of the web site that you wish to visit.

 Unlike Internet Explorer, you can't use the mouse to click one time inside the Safari web address box to instantly "highlight" the current web address.

To *highlight* the current web address with the mouse in Safari, you have to click inside the Safari address box **multiple times** in quick succession (knock knock knock!):

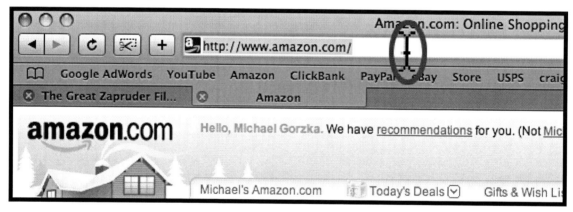

 A much simpler way (in your author's humble opinion) is to **hold down** the "command" key and then press the "L" key on your Apple computer keyboard one time.

command + L keyboard shortcut

This will instantly *highlight* the current web address in the Safari web address box.

After the current web address has been highlighted, you can type in the web address of the web site that you wish to visit and then press the "return" key on your keyboard one time.

SAFARI "TABS"

The Safari web browser (like Firefox and IE 7) features *tabbed* web browsing.

"Tabs" enable you to have more than one web page open at the same time in a **single** window:

Safari "Tabs" (circled)

You can *switch* between open tabs by clicking the tab containing the web page that you wish to view.

How to Open a New Tab

To open a new tab, you can select "New Tab" from the Safari "File" menu:

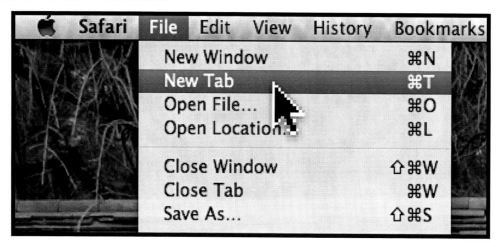

 You can also open a new tab by holding down the "command" key and then pressing the "T" key one time.

Once a new tab is opened, you can type a web address into the tab's web address box (circled in the following picture) and then press the "return" key one time.

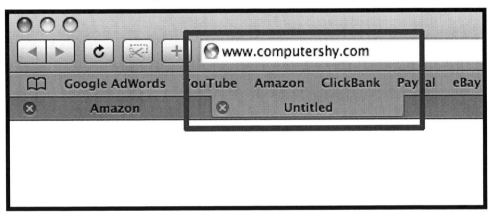

You will then have **two** Safari tabs open (each containing a different web page):

How to Open a Link in a New Tab

First open the Safari *preferences* window by selecting "Preferences" from the "Safari" menu and click "Tabs" at the top of the preferences window:

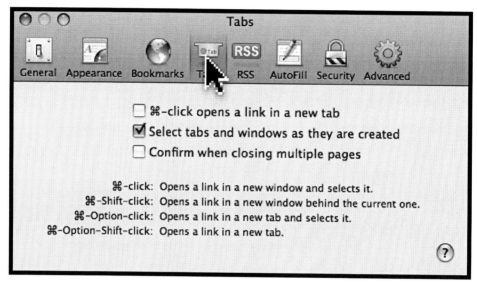

Use the mouse to check the *command-click opens a link in a new tab* checkbox:

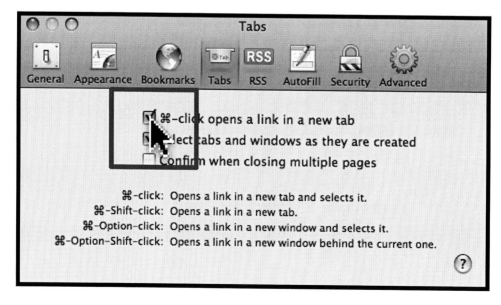

You can now open a link in a **new tab** by holding down the "command" key on the keyboard as you click the link:

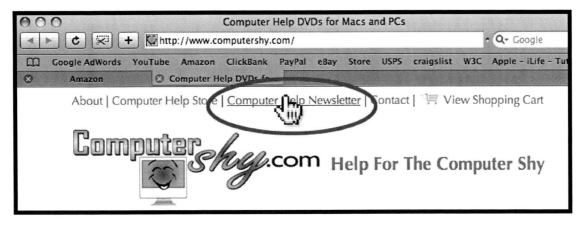

This will open the web page that the link leads to in a new tab:

How to Close a Tab

You can *close* a tab by using the mouse to click the little "x" on the tab that you wish to close:

You can hold down the "command" key and press the "w" key one time to close the tab that is currently open.

If you *hold down* the "option" key (on the bottom row of your keyboard) as you are clicking on a tab's close button ('x'), *all* open tabs will close **except** the tab that you are "option-clicking" on.

SAFARI "BOOKMARKS"

 Safari Bookmarks work exactly like the Web page "Favorites" in Internet Explorer.

There are two places for Safari "Bookmarks":

1. the bookmarks "bar"

2. the bookmarks "menu"

Bookmarks Bar

The bookmarks **bar** is for web pages that you visit frequently and want easy access to:

To visit any of the web pages on your bookmarks bar, you can use the mouse to click the bookmark that you wish to visit:

 You can also hold down the "command" key and then press the "number" of the bookmark that you wish to visit.

For example, on my bookmarks bar pictured here:

If I wanted to visit Amazon (the *first* bookmark on my bookmarks bar), I would hold down the "command" key and press the number **1** key on my keyboard.

How to add a bookmark to the Safari bookmarks "bar"

1) To add a web page to your bookmark "bar", you can click the plus sign (+) on the Safari toolbar:

You can also hold down the "command" key and press the "d" key one time:

Either action will cause a bookmark "window" to appear:

Please note in the above picture that "Computer Help DVDs for Macs and PCs" is *highlighted*.

This means that you **do not** have to click inside that box first in order to type in a different name for that bookmark.

2) Type short (but descriptive) names for the bookmarks on your bookmarks bar to save space.

3) After you have typed a new name for your bookmark, use the mouse to select "Bookmarks Bar" from the drop-down menu box:

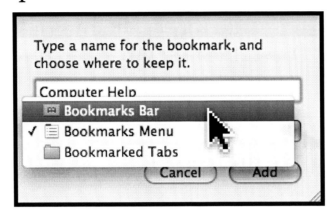

4) Finally, click the "Add" button one time:

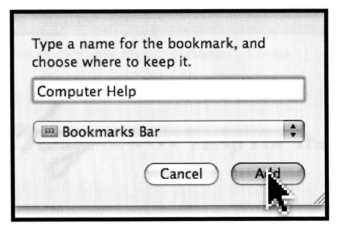

This will **add** the web page you are currently on to your bookmarks bar:

Add a web page to the bookmarks "menu"

The Safari "Bookmarks" menu works the same way as the Internet Explorer "Favorites" menu.

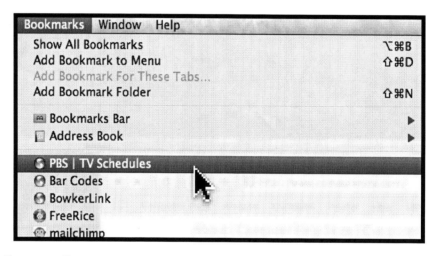

To add a web page to your Bookmarks Menu, follow the preceding procedure but select "Bookmarks Menu" from the drop-down menu box:

GOOGLE SEARCH BOX

 *Internet Explorer 7* has a "Windows Live" search box at the top right corner of the window.

Apple Safari has a Google search box at the top right corner of the window:

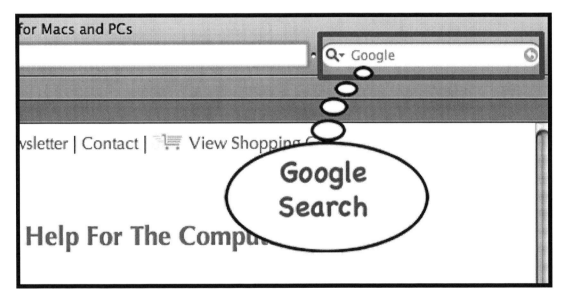

This box enables you to search **Google** from any web page that you are currently on.

You do *not* have to go to www.google.com to perform a Google search (not that there's anything wrong with that).

How to use the Safari Google Search box

First you need to get the "blinking line" (text insertion point) into the Google search box:

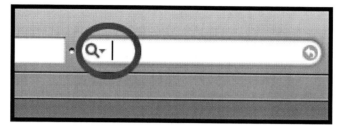

To do this you can either use the mouse to click inside the search box **or** press the "option", "command", and the "f" keys all at the same time:

Once the *blinking line* is in the Google search box, you can type what you are looking for:

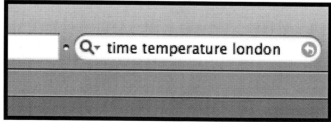

After you have typed your search words into the Google search box, press the "return" key on your keyboard one time.

This will take you to a Google search results page:

 Once you are on the Web there are no differences between Macs & PCs.

The "Back" Button

The "Back" Button is located at the top left corner of the Safari Web browser:

You can click the "Back" button to *return* to the web page that you were most previously on.

You can also press the larger "delete" key on the upper right side of your Apple computer keyboard to return to a previous web page.

You will **not** be able to use this keyboard shortcut if the "blinking line" is in a text box on a web page:

The iCal Program

The fun & very useful iCal program does not (to the best of my knowledge) have a Windows equivalent.

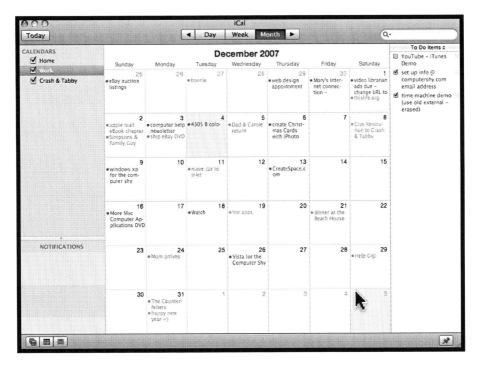

You can use iCal to keep track of your various appointments; set reminder alarms; open files at designated times; create "To Do" lists; and more.

In short, you can have iCal tell you what you have to do and when you have to do it.

ICAL DEMONSTRATION

I have an appointment coming up in which I have to help one of my "computer shy" friends set up her Internet connection.

How to Start the iCal Program

You can start the iCal program by single-clicking its icon on the program dock:

How to set an iCal "event"

After the iCal program starts you can select a daily, weekly, or monthly *view* of your calendar of events:

If you have to set an appointment for later in the month, start with the "Month" view.

Use the mouse to click one time on the day that you wish to set the "event" for:

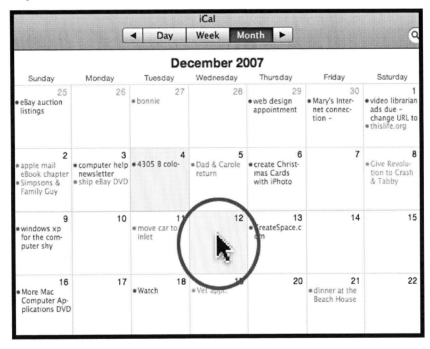

Then use the mouse to click the "Day" button near the top of the iCal window:

This will cause the "Day" view of the date that you selected to appear.

Use the mouse to double-click on the time of the event. In this example that time is **10 AM**:

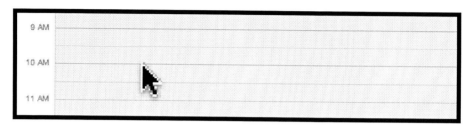

This will cause an "event" bar to appear for that time:

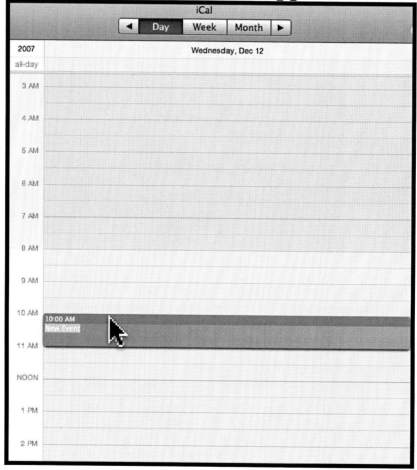

In the above picture, the words "New Event" in the event bar are *highlighted*.

This means that you can type in a **description** of your "event" (*without* having to click inside the box first):

After you have typed in the description for your event, use the mouse to *double-click* the event box:

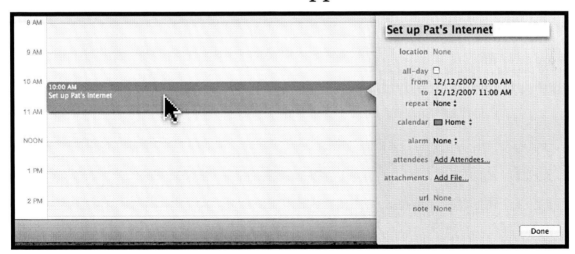

This will cause a window to appear for that event:

You can use this window to provide yourself with all the necessary info about the "event" and set an alarm.

Event Window Functions

- Revise the description
- Reset the time(s)
- Select a calendar (if you have more than one)
- Set an alarm
- Open a file
- And more!

First I'm going to add "Verizon" to the event description:

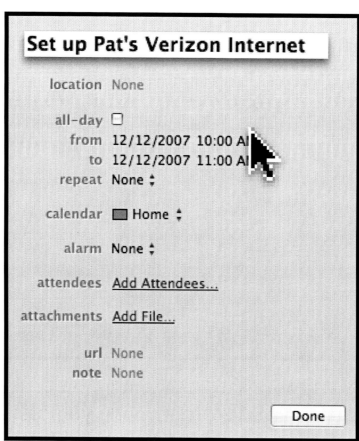

Pat lives right next door so I'll skip over the "location" field.

I figure this "event" will take about 2 hours so I'll change "to" from 11:00 AM to 12 PM:

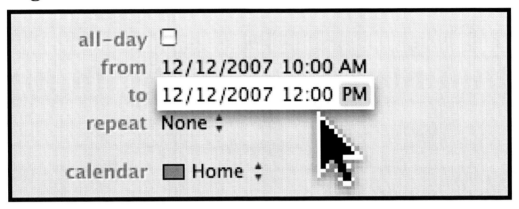

I have three calendars on my iCal program (one for home stuff, one for my cats, and the other for my "Help for the Computer Shy" activities).

This appointment falls into the third category (i.e. "work") so I'll select that from the "calendar" menu:

I would like a *sound message* to appear to remind me when it's time for my Internet setup appointment so

I'll select "Message with sound" from the "alarm" menu:

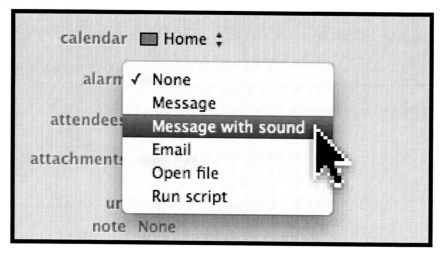

Select the *time* for the alarm message to appear (30 minutes before the "event" in this example):

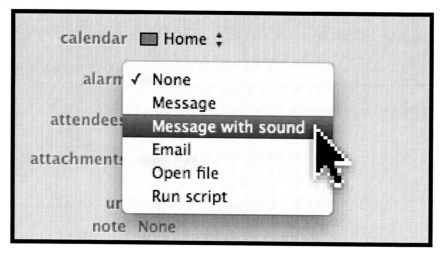

I also have a document with Pat's Internet setup information saved on my Mac computer hard drive.

I would like that Internet setup document to *automatically* open 30 minutes before the time of the appointment --- so **in addition** to the "message with sound" alarm, I will set up an *"Open file"* alarm for this event.

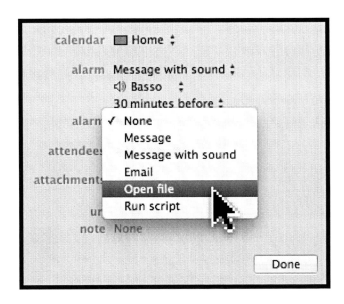

The only thing left to do is to click the "Done" button at the lower right corner of the "event" window.

The visual demonstrations for this chapter are prefaced by "iCal" at http://gallery.mac.com/ help4computershy

The Apple Address Book

The **Address Book** program is pretty self-explanatory. It contains and organizes contact information for the various businesses, organizations and people in your life.

The Address Book also neatly ties into your Apple Mail program *and* the Google Maps program.

HOW TO START THE ADDRESS BOOK

You can start the Address Book program by single-clicking its icon on the program dock:

The icon will bounce a few times and then the program will start.

TIP: If you already have programs open, you can select *Hide others* from the "Address Book" menu so that the other programs will not be visible.

HOW TO ADD A CONTACT

Click the "Create a new card" button near the bottom left corner of the Address Book window:

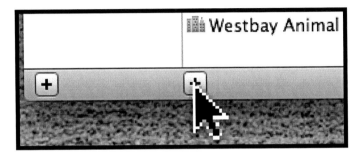

This will cause a blank "card" to appear on the right side of the Address Book window:

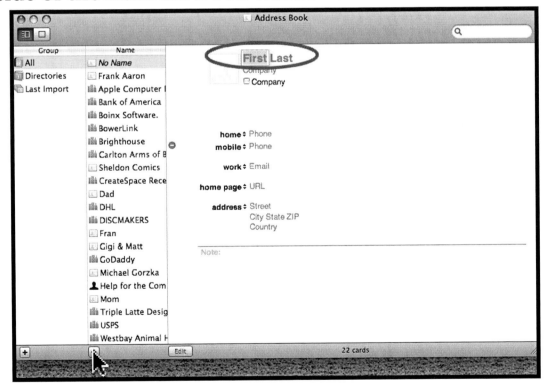

Please note in the above picture that the "First" box is *highlighted.*

This means that you can type in the contact's first name (*without* having to click inside that box first):

What if the Address Book "card" I'm creating is for a company or organization rather than a person?

Use the mouse to check the "Company" checkbox:

This will immediately change the "person" card into a "company" card:

To fill out a *field* on an Address Book card, use the mouse to click inside the field that you wish to fill out:

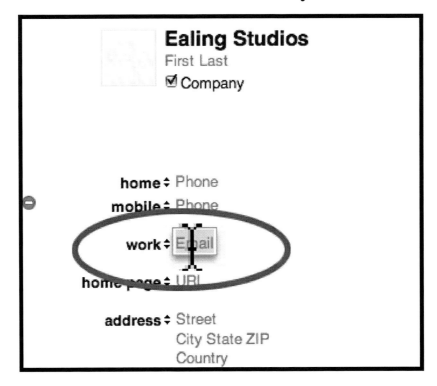

After the field has been *highlighted*, you can type into it:

After you have completed the card for your new contact (or have filled out all the fields that you wish to fill out), use the mouse to click the "edit" button at the bottom of the **Address Book** window:

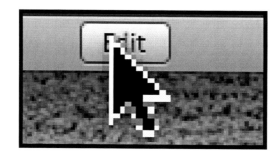

THE APPLE MAIL / ADDRESS BOOK CONNECTION

One of the many great thing about Mac computers is how the various programs on a Mac work together seamlessly.

Once you have entered somebody's email address into your Apple **Address Book**, you will no longer need to type their email address into the "To" box of the Apple **Mail** program.

For example, Frank Aaron is in my Address book. So if I want to email him, all I have to do is to type "Frank" into the *To* box:

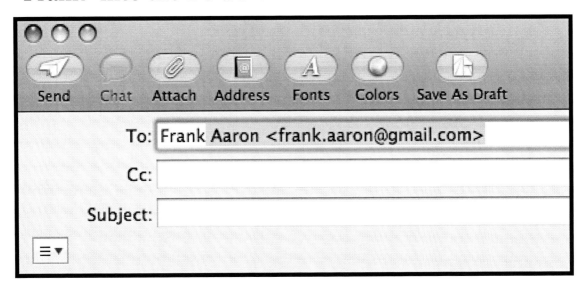

As soon I typed "Frank" into the **To** box, the **Mail** program automatically retrieved Frank's email address from the **Address Book** and typed it into the "To" box for me.

 The online "Address Book" movie demonstrates how you can add the *sender* of an email message to your **Address Book** with just a couple mouse clicks.

iTunes Program

- How to Start iTunes
- The iTunes Store
- Your iTunes Account
- How to Browse the iTunes Store
- How to Download a Song
- How to Play Songs
- iTunes Playlists

The Apple iTunes program rates a book and/or DVD program all by itself.

In a nutshell, you can use the iTunes program to download (and organize) music, videos, movies, podcasts, & audiobooks.

You can also use iTunes to *import* your own CDs. This is useful if you would like to have all of your music and audiobooks in the same place (and *even more useful* if you are planning to transfer your audio collection to your iPod).

My friend is driving from Florida to Alaska so he put all his music CDs onto his iPod so he can listen to them on his trip --- and never have to listen to the same song twice!

This chapter provides an overview of the iTunes program. It is by no means comprehensive but should be enough to get you started.

 If you are interested in a more in-depth look at the iTunes program, please check out our "*More* Mac Computer Applications for the Computer Shy" instructional DVD.

 If you have used the iTunes program for Windows then you should be all set to use iTunes for Mac. Both programs work the same way.

HOW TO START THE ITUNES PROGRAM

Use the mouse to click the iTunes icon on the program dock one time:

THE ITUNES STORE

You can visit the iTunes store by using the mouse to click "iTunes Store" on the left side of the iTunes window:

Your Mac computer must be connected to the Internet to access the iTunes store.

As I said earlier, the online Apple iTunes store has a lot to offer.

Once you have entered the iTunes store, you can browse (or *search*) for songs, movies, audiobooks, free podcasts, and more.

The Apple iTunes Store

HOW TO BROWSE THE ITUNES STORE

You can *browse* the iTunes store by categories (start with a broad category and then "drill down" to the specific sub-category that you are looking for).

For example if you are looking for Classical music, you can first click "Browse" on the right side of the iTunes window.

After you have clicked on the "Browse" link, you can select the genre of music that you are interested in:

You can then select a "Subgenre":

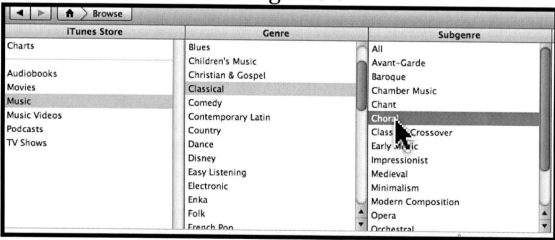

 Please note the scroll bars on each column window. You may have to scroll down the window to see everything that's in it.

After you have selected a subgenre, you can then select a recording artist (and an album from that recording artist) within that subgenre:

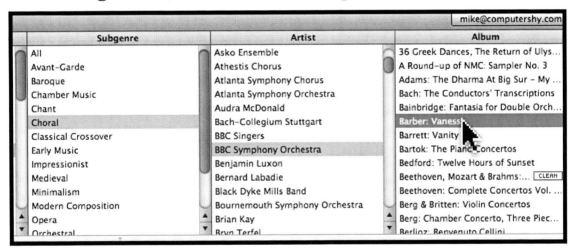

ITUNES STORE NAVIGATION BUTTONS

Near the top left corner of the iTunes window, you will see some navigation buttons:

These buttons ("back", "forward", and "home") are similar to the same buttons on a web browser.

You can click the "back" and "forward" buttons to *retrace* your iTunes store browsing steps.

You can also click the "home" button to start all over again (i.e. return to the iTunes Store home page).

HOW TO SEARCH THE ITUNES STORE

Browsing is great if you just want to see what the iTunes store has for a particular subgenre or recording artist.

If you are looking for something in particular (such as a specific album, movie, recording artist, song, or audiobook) you can use the iTunes store *search box*.

The search box is located at the top right corner of the iTunes window:

If you are interested in a particular singer, album title, conductor, or audiobook author, you can type what you are looking for into the *Search iTunes Store* box:

After you have typed what you are looking for into the *Search iTunes Store* box, press the "return" key on your keyboard one time.

This will take you to a search results page:

You can purchase musical works by album (as shown above) or by song:

	Name		Time	Artist		Album			Price	
1	Sleep	⊙	5:33	Polyphony & Ste...	⊙	Whitacre: Cloud...	⊙		$0.99	BUY SONG
2	Lux aurumque	⊙	4:08	Polyphony & Ste...	⊙	Whitacre: Cloud...	⊙		$0.99	BUY SONG
3	Cloudburst	⊙	8:25	Polyphony & Ste...	⊙	Whitacre: Cloud...	⊙		$0.99	BUY SONG
4	Water Night	⊙	5:03	Polyphony & Ste...	⊙	Whitacre: Cloud...	⊙		$0.99	BUY SONG

 You can *preview* a song before you buy it by double-clicking its title.

YOUR ITUNES ACCOUNT

Before you can purchase or download anything from the Apple iTunes store, you will have to set up an account.

 The procedure for signing up for an iTunes store account is pretty straightforward. You will need a credit card or debit card however.

First use the mouse to click the "Sign In" button at the top right corner of the iTunes window:

This will cause a screen to appear that enables you to either sign into your existing account or create a new one.

If you already have an *Apple ID*, you can enter it into the Apple ID box (if not, type your email address):

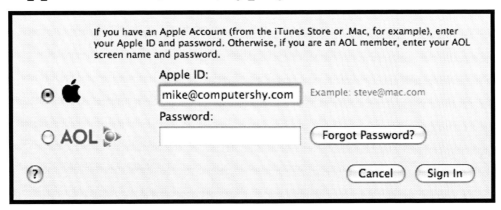

You can create a *new account* by clicking the "Create New Account" button:

All you have to do to set up a new iTunes account is to fill out a few forms and provide your credit or debit card information.

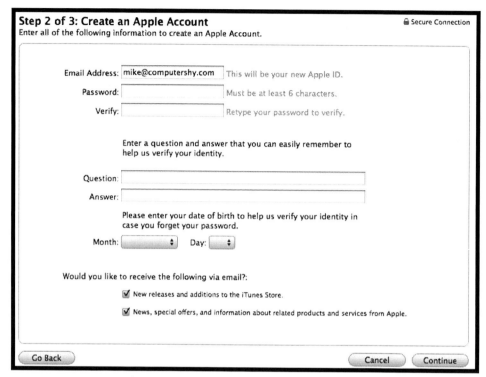

Step 2 of 3: Create an Apple Account 🔒 Secure Connection
Enter all of the following information to create an Apple Account.

Email Address: mike@computershy.com   This will be your new Apple ID.

Password: [   ]   Must be at least 6 characters.

Verify: [   ]   Retype your password to verify.

Enter a question and answer that you can easily remember to help us verify your identity.

Question: [   ]

Answer: [   ]

Please enter your date of birth to help us verify your identity in case you forget your password.

Month: [▼]   Day: [▼]

Would you like to receive the following via email?:

☑ New releases and additions to the iTunes Store.

☑ News, special offers, and information about related products and services from Apple.

(Go Back)   (Cancel) (Continue)

iTunes Account Signup Form

The entire sign-up process takes about 5 minutes.

Please take your time when you are completing these forms and remember your security question and answer.

By the way, Apple has had my credit card and other personal information on file for the last 7 years and I have never had any problems (such as identity theft or fraudulent charges) resulting from that.

HOW TO "DOWNLOAD" A SONG

After you have set up your iTunes account, all you have to do to purchase and download a song (or Audiobook, TV show, movie, etc) is to click the "Buy" button opposite the item that you wish to purchase:

	Name	Time	Artist	Album		Price		Popularity
1	Christmas Time Is Here (Instru...	6:07	Vince Guaraldi T...	A Charlie Brown ...		$0.99	BUY SONG	
2	Linus & Lucy	3:08	Vince Guaraldi T...	A Charlie Brown ...		$0.99	BUY SONG	
3	Christmastime Is Here (Vocal)	2:47	Vince Guaraldi T...	A Charlie Brown ...		$0.99	BUY SONG	
4	Christmas Time Is Here (Vocal ...	2:45	Vince Guaraldi T...	A Charlie Brown ...		$0.99	BUY SONG	
5	O Tannenbaum	5:11	Vince Guaraldi T...	A Charlie Brown ...		$0.99	BUY SONG	
6	Linus and Lucy	3:06	Vince Guaraldi T...	A Charlie Brown ...		$0.99	BUY SONG	
7	Christmastime Is Here (Instru...	6:08	Vince Guaraldi T...	A Charlie Brown ...		$0.99	BUY SONG	
8	Christmas Is Coming	3:25	Vince Guaraldi T...	A Charlie Brown ...		$0.99	BUYING	
9	Please Come Home for Christ...	2:53	Jon Bon Jovi	A Very Special C...		$0.99	BUYING	

HOW TO PLAY SONGS

First use the mouse to open your Music folder by clicking the "Music" folder near the top left corner of the iTunes window.

This will display all the songs that you have either *downloaded* or *imported* into your iTunes program.

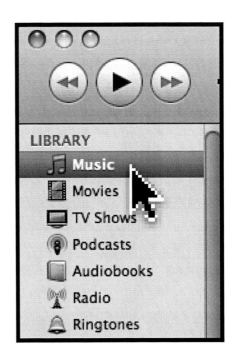

iTunes Account Music Library

To play any of these songs, use the mouse to *double-click* the song that you wish to play:

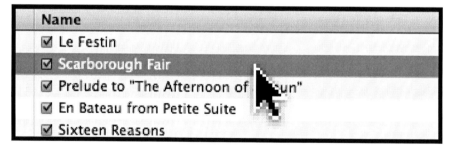

 You can play items in your Audiobooks & Podcasts folders using the same procedure (only first select one of those folders instead of your "Music" folder).

iTunes Controls

At the top left corner of your iTunes window you will some controls:

If you have ever used a stereo of any kind, these controls will be self-explanatory.

For example, you can click the "Pause" button (||) to *pause* the iTunes track you are playing.

Please keep in mind that the iTunes volume control and your Mac's volume control are not the same.

In other words, if you *mute* your Mac computer, you can crank the volume control on your iTunes program all the way up and still not hear a thing.

 Apple computers have built-in speakers but they really aren't suitable for playing music.

You may want to invest in a pair of external speakers if you are going to be listening to music and/or viewing movies on your Mac computer.

External speakers aren't very expensive and they can really enhance your Mac computer experiences.

ITUNES PLAYLISTS

You can *organize* the music in your iTunes *Music* folder into "Playlists":

Let's say that you *import* one of your music CDs into your iTunes library and you want to create a *playlist* for that album.

NOTE: If you place a music CD into your Mac computer, iTunes will *automatically* import the music from that CD in your iTunes music library.

First use the mouse to click the "Create a Playlist" button at the lower left corner of your iTunes window:

This will cause a **new** untitled *playlist* to appear:

Please note in the above picture that the words "untitled playlist" are *highlighted.*

This means that you can *immediately* type in a name for your newly created playlist:

How to Copy Songs to a Playlist

1) First use the mouse to click on the song that you wish to *copy* to the playlist:

Name	Time
☑ Le Festin	2:51
☑ Scarborough Fair	3:13
☑ Prelude to "The Afternoon of a Faun"	8:28
☑ En Bateau from Pe Suite	3:46
☑ Sixteen Reasons	1:58

TIP: You can hold down the *command* key on your keyboard to select more than one song at the same time:

Name		Time
☑ Le Festin		2:51
☑ Scarborough Fair		3:13
☑ Prelude to "The Afternoon of a Faun"	➔	8:28
☑ En Bateau from Petite Suite		3:46
☑ Sixteen Reasons		1:58
☑ Lyric Pieces	➔	1:14
☑ Blue Horizon	➔	6:05
☑ Eternal Wave		14:31
☑ Light of the Moon	➔	14:08
☑ Celestial Glow		14:12
☑ Water Voices	➔	11:43
☑ Thunderstorm In The Wilderness		51:02
☑ Thunderstorm In The Wilderness		51:02
☑ Wouldn't It Be Good		3:45

You can also hold down the "shift" key to select a *range* of songs:

Name		Time
☑ Le Festin		2:51
☑ Scarborough Fair		3:13
☑ Prelude to "The Afternoon of a Faun"	➔	8:28
☑ En Bateau from Petite Suite	➔	3:46
☑ Sixteen Reasons	➔	1:58
☑ Lyric Pieces	➔	1:14
☑ Blue Horizon	➔	6:05
☑ Eternal Wave	➔	14:31
☑ Light of the Moon	➔	14:08
☑ Celestial Glow	➔	14:12
☑ Water Voices	➔	11:43
☑ Thunderstorm In The Wilderness		51:02
☑ Thunderstorm In The Wilderness		51:02
☑ Wouldn't It Be Good		3:45

2) After you have selected the songs that you wish to *copy* from your main music folder to your playlist, use the mouse to place the tip of the screen arrow over one of the songs that you have selected:

Name		Time
☑ Le Festin		2:51
☑ Scarborough Fair		3:13
☑ Prelude to "The Afternoon of a Faun"	●	8:28
☑ Bateau from Petite Suite	●	3:46
☑ teen Reasons	●	1:58
☑ Lyric Pieces	●	1:14
☑ Blue Horizon	●	6:05
☑ Eternal Wave	●	14:31
☑ Light of the Moon	●	14:08
☑ Celestial Glow	●	14:12
☑ Water Voices	●	11:43

3) Press and *hold down* the mouse button (do not "click" the mouse).

4) As you are holding the mouse button down, move the mouse on the mousepad in the direction(s) of the playlist that you wish to copy them to:

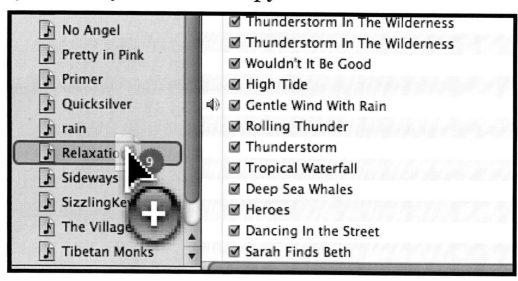

5) When the song(s) that you are dragging are *directly over* the playlist, stop moving the mouse on the mousepad and release the mouse button that you had been holding down.

6) Open the playlist that you just dragged the songs to by clicking its name one time (left side of the iTunes window):

How to "Burn" a Playlist to a CD

This is really simple! There's just three steps here:

1. Open the playlist that you wish to burn to a CD

2. Insert a blank CD-R into your Mac's *CD drive*

3. Click the "Burn Disc" button at the lower right corner of the iTunes window

 A video demonstration showing how a playlist is created and then *burned* to a CD is prefaced by "iTunes" on http://gallery.mac.com/help4computershy.

Dashboard Widgets

- What are widgets?
- How do I get to my widgets?
- What can widgets do for me?
- How do I install additional dashboard widgets?

WHAT ARE WIDGETS?

"Widgets" are tiny programs (mostly free of charge) that you can download and install onto your Mac's "Dashboard".

Your Mac comes equipped with some basic dashboard widgets (such as a calculator widget, a dictionary widget and a clock widget) but you can download many more if you like.

Dashboard Widgets

HOW DO I GET TO MY DASHBOARD WIDGETS?

To see (and use) your dashboard widgets, you can use the mouse to click the "Dashboard" icon on your program dock:

 A much quicker way to access your dashboard widgets is to press the "F12" key on your computer keyboard.

 What can these "widgets" do for me?

 There are widgets for most anything!

If you can think of a subject, chances are there will be a widget for it.

 Widgets are for the most part free (but some widgets are "shareware" meaning that you have to pay for them at some point).

Common Widget Functions

- Time & Temperature (in any locale you designate)
- Weather forecast
- Calculator
- Sticky Notes
- Unit Conversion
- Address Lookup
- Where the cheapest gas is in your neighborhood
- Games (a lot of them!)

 How do I install other dashboard widgets?

 There are two places where you can find and install additional dashboard widgets for your Mac:

1. From your dashboard archive

2. From www.apple.com/downloads/dashboard/

Your Dashboard Widget "Archive"

To see the other dashboard widgets that came with your Mac computer, first press the **F12** key on your keyboard one time:

This will cause your dashboard widgets to appear:

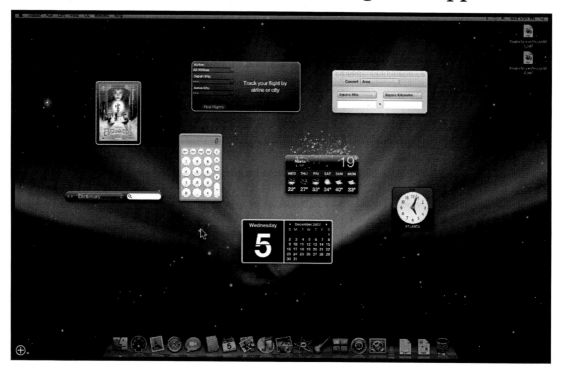

Then use the mouse to click the plus sign (+) at the lower left corner of your computer screen:

This will cause your dashboard widgets "bin" to appear at the very bottom of your computer screen:

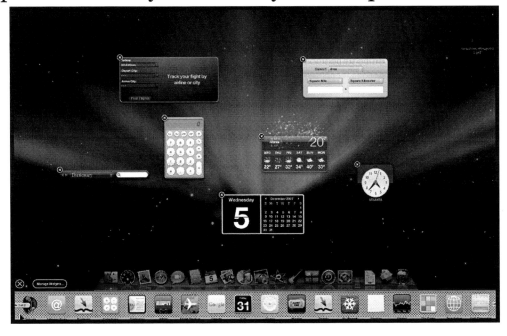

 If you click the mouse or press any keys on your keyboard, the widgets will disappear (and you will have to press the **F12** key again to get them to come back).

Use the mouse to click the "Manage Widgets" button at the lower left corner of your computer screen:

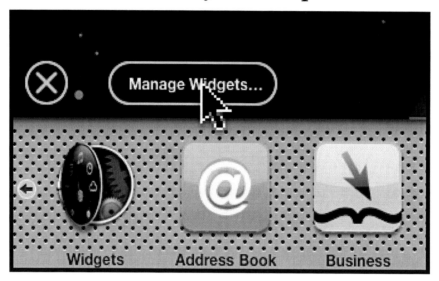

This will cause your "Manage Widgets" window to appear:

Please note the *scroll bar* in the following picture. You can scroll up and down this window to see all the widgets currently installed on your Mac.

You can *double-click* any of the widgets in the widgets window to add it to your widgets dashboard:

How to Remove a Widget From Your Dashboard

1. Press the **F12** key on your keyboard to cause your widgets to appear.
2. Click the plus sign (+) at the lower left corner of your computer screen (as previously described).

3.   Click the plus sign at the upper left corner of the widget that you wish to remove from your widget dashboard:

HOW TO GET MORE DASHBOARD WIDGETS

New Dashboard Widgets become available on a daily basis.

Some you will find to be useful; others widgets will look like fun; and some will be just plain *weird*.

To "shop" for new and exciting widgets...

First point your Apple Safari web browser to www.apple.com/downloads/dashboard/:

This will bring you to the dashboard widgets page:

Please note in the above picture that you can browse widgets by "Categories", "Just Added", and "Top 50".

Most of the widgets that you find here will be free of charge.

Some widget owners request a donation ("Donationware") and some widget providers will let you use a widget for a length of time before requesting a fee ("Shareware").

Download Details

Company: **baKno games**

Version: **1.5**

Post Date: **November 26, 2007**

License: Shareware

File Size: **4.5MB**

URL Type: **Download**

Download ID: **16181**

Please read any information provided about the widget before you download it.

Most of the widgets that you will find on this page are **not** made by Apple, Inc.

I have been downloading widgets to my Mac for the last two years or so. None of them have ever harmed my Mac or impaired its functionality in any way.

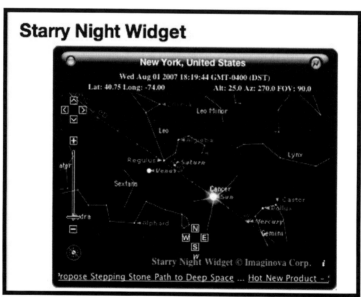

Widgets do not take up very much space on your Mac's hard drive.

I also have never heard of any widgets causing harm to anybody else's Mac Computer.

That being said, please use your best judgement when selecting which widgets to download.

It's probably best to avoid widgets that make unrealistic claims, for example.

Widget Download & Installation Procedure

1) After you have found a widget that you wish to have on your widget dashboard, use the mouse to click its "Download" button.

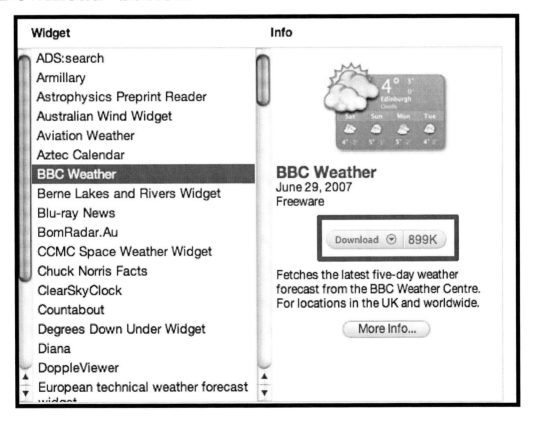

NOTE: You can also click the "More Info" link to learn more about the widget and the makers of that widget.

Clicking a widget's download link will cause your
Safari "Downloads" window to appear:

A "Widget Installer" window will also appear asking if
you *really* want to install this widget on your
Dashboard:

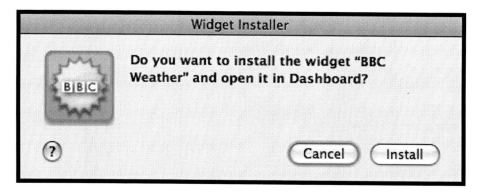

NOTE: Whenever a window such as this appears,
carefully read the information on that window before
you click anything.

The Widget Installer window is a **security** feature of the Mac Operating system.

2) To install the widget on your Mac, click the "Install" button on the Widget Installer window.

Your dashboard widgets will then appear along with the new widget that you just downloaded.

3) Use the mouse to click the "Keep" button on your new widget and you're done!

You can press the **F12** key on your keyboard to cause your dashboard widgets to appear. Press the **F12** key on your keyboard to make them disappear.

You can also click the *Dashboard* icon on your Mac's program dock to toggle your dashboard widgets on and off.

Mac Printer Setup

This going to be a very short chapter because setting up a printer for your Mac is about as complicated as throwing a pair of socks into a drawer.

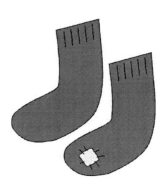

HOW TO *BUY* A PRINTER FOR YOUR MAC

To be honest, I can't really recommend one printer over another.

I've used all the brand names (Canon, HP, Lexmark, Epson, et al) and they all produced serviceable printouts.

But I can give you some general tips:

- Buy a **USB** printer for your Mac (Look for the *USB Logo* on the printer's box or product description)
- Buy a brand name (beware cheap knockoffs)

- Find out the prices for the **print cartridges** (that's where the *real cost* of owning your own printer is)
- Check out Amazon.com (they usually offer free shipping and some pretty good discounts and / or rebates)

HOW TO *SET UP* A PRINTER FOR YOUR MAC

 Even if you are using the *Parallels* or *Fusion* programs to run "Windows" on your Mac, here's the procedure to connect a USB printer to your Mac.

1) Carefully follow the *set up* instructions that came with your USB printer:

2) Plug one end of the USB cable into your printer:

3) Plug the other end of the USB cable into the USB "port" on your Mac Computer:

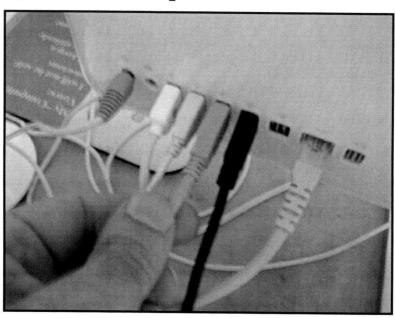

 The USB port on your computer will have this symbol next to it:

4) Turn your printer **on** by pressing its power button.

 That's pretty much it! Your Mac should automatically sense the connected USB printer.

5) Fire up your Mac's *TextEdit* program and print a test page.

If your Mac does *not* detect your printer, check the USB cable connections (twice) and then restart your Mac.

 What about the "Windows" side of my Mac?

Answer

Since this is a **USB** printer, the "Windows" side of your Mac computer will *also* automatically detect it.

Remember that USB may officially stand for "Universal Serial Bus" but it really means "Plug and Play".

Each month in the "Help for the Computer Shy" newsletter, we publish additional tips, tutorials, and resources to help Macs and PCs get along.

www.computershy.com/news

How to open Windows Files on Your Mac

 The really good news is that *you may not need to install Windows on your Mac computer.*

In fact, my advice is to **avoid** doing so if at all possible.

You can accomplish pretty much anything on your Mac computer without resorting to Parallels or Fusion.

If there is a particular program that you were using on Windows, chances are there is a Mac program on the market that will do the very same thing for you.

Besides, Windows and Mac computers are actually pretty compatible these days.

If one of your Windows-using comrades sends you a file to open, there's a good chance that you'll be able to do so without difficulty.

Yes, you may need to buy additional software for your Mac such as the *iWork* software package (which is the

Apple equivalent of Microsoft Office) but this will be easier, cheaper and *safer* than installing virus and spyware susceptible Windows on your pristine Mac.

I'll tell you what. Before you install Windows on your Mac, email me first: mike@computershy.com.

HOW TO OPEN A WINDOWS DOCUMENT ON YOUR MAC

Okay, let's say that someone just sent you an important Windows document and you don't have that particular Windows program (or its Mac equivalent), what are you going to to do?

First double-click the file:

If your Mac has an appropriate program to open the file with, it will automatically do so.

If the file does *not* automatically open, here's what you can do:

1. "Control-click" on the Windows file

2. Select "Open With" from the pop-up menu

3. Select "Other" from the "Open With" sub-menu:

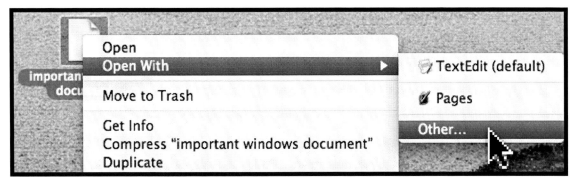

This will cause a "Choose Application" window to appear containing all the programs / applications on your Mac:

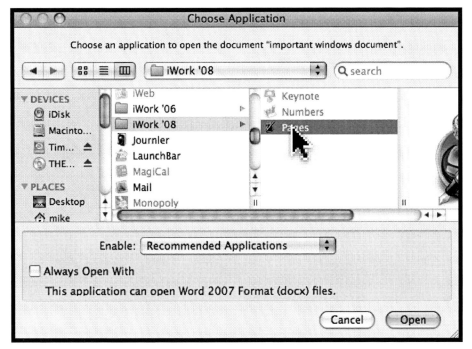

You can use the mouse to select various applications from this window to open the Windows file with.

If *none* of the applications on your Mac are able to open the Windows file, you will probably have to buy additional software for your Mac.

But please <u>email me</u> first!

Front Row

A surprising fact is that your Mac actually doubles as a pretty gosh darn good home entertainment system.

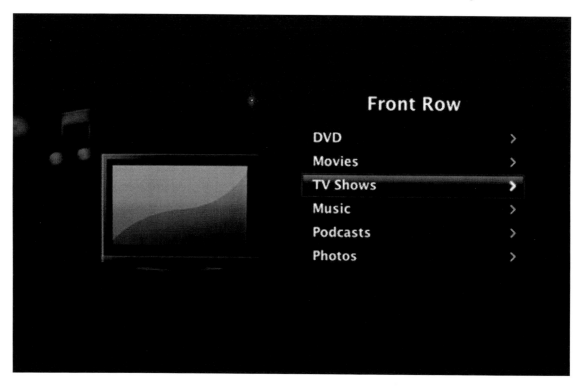

 In a nutshell, you can use the "Front Row" program to play whatever you download (or import) into your Apple *iTunes* program or your *iPhoto* program:

- Movies
- TV shows
- Podcasts
- Music
- Photos
- University classes (via iTunes U)

The Front Row program can be controlled with an Apple Remote (included with newer Mac computers):

This remote has 6 buttons and is very easy to use.

Couch jockeys rejoice! You can play movies (and everything else on the previous list) without getting up.

To cause your Mac's *Front Row* program to appear, simply point the remote toward your Mac and press the "Menu" button one time.

Once the stylish *Front Row* interface appears, you can switch between the various multimedia sources on your Mac computer (DVD drive, movies folder, photos folder, etc) by pressing the *plus* and *minus* signs on the remote:

Once you have started a movie, a podcast, a TV show, or song, you can adjust the *volume* with those same plus and minus buttons.

Please invest in a pair of external speakers for your Mac. They'll make a world of difference and you can get a good pair for under $100.00. I have found some very good deals on Amazon.com and eBay.

The Front Row remote control is *magnetic*. You can affix it to the lower right corner of your iMac computer:

The remote control is about the size of pack of chewing gum (and weighs about the same).

I would have lost my remote years ago without its handy magnetic quality.

You can also start the *Front Row* program from your keyboard by pressing the *esc* key (top left corner) one time as you are *holding down* one of the "command" keys.

THE DVD PLAYER

If you insert a movie DVD into your Mac's Disk Drive:

The Apple DVD player will automatically take over and play the DVD for you:

Regrettably, the Apple DVD player *cannot* be controlled with the Apple Remote (not yet anyway).

Here's what you can do to control your DVD movies (from your couch!) with your Apple remote...

1. Put the DVD movie into your Mac's Disk Drive

2. Close the DVD Player program ("command + Q" keyboard shortcut)

3. Press the "Menu" button on your Apple remote.

4. Press the **+** and **−** buttons on the remote to select "DVD" from the Front Row menu.

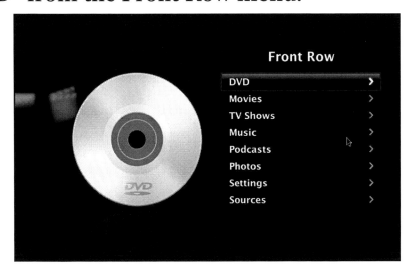

You will now be able to use the Apple remote to control the playing of the DVD (pause, stop, fast forward, volume control, etc.)

Time Saving Mac Keyboard Shortcuts

Keyboard command	Action
command + q	quit program
command + w	close window
Shift-command-Delete	empty trash (when "Finder" is active program)
command + s	save
option + command + h	hide other programs
command + n	new "Finder" window
command + delete	send selected item to Trash
command + z	"undo" last action

Keyboard command	Action
command + x	"cut"
command + c	"copy"
command +v	"paste"

Your "Downloads" Folder

If you are using Mac OS 10.5 (aka "Leopard"), **by default** (*unless* you specify a different folder on your Mac) any file that you save or "download" to your Mac will land in your *Downloads* folder.

The Downloads folder has a shortcut icon on your Mac program dock --- just to the left of the Trash Can:

1) To see your "downloads", use the mouse to click the shortcut icon for the Downloads folder on the program dock one time.

As soon as you click the "Downloads" folder, you will see thumbnail images of everything in your Downloads folder (right now I only have a single picture in my Downloads folder).

2) To open your Downloads folder, click the "Open in Finder" button which will appear *directly above* the preview images:

Your *Downloads* folder will open in a window just like any other folder on your Mac.

Where to go From Here

First and foremost, use your Mac computer and have a good time.

You can do a lot of fun, exciting, and interesting things with your new Mac buddy.

If you have any questions about the material that we covered here or would like some additional video demonstrations, I'm only an <u>email</u> away.

Please visit <u>www.computershy.com</u> for free updates to this book and for more Mac computer help manuals and instructional DVDs.

All of our computer help products come with free updates and a money back guarantee.

While you are perusing our Mac computer help offerings, please sign up for our free <u>Help for the Computer Shy newsletter</u>.

Each month we publish tips, tutorials, and resources to help you best take advantage of everything that your Mac computer has to offer.

You'll also be notified of book updates and when additional visual demonstrations are posted.

Thank you so much for reading this book! I sincerely hope that you found it to be useful and that you thoroughly enjoy your Mac computer adventures.

Michael Gorzka

Help for the Computer Shy

<u>www.computershy.com</u>

<u>mike@computershy.com</u>

864891